PENG

## THE WEALTHY BANKER'S WIFE

In her seventeen years as a journalist, Linda McQuaig has covered a wide range of subjects, from the revolution in Iran to the financial dealings of Canada's establishment.

She has worked for *Maclean's* magazine, CBC Radio and the *Globe and Mail,* where she was most recently a national political reporter. Her investigation of what became known as the Patti Starr scandal won her a National Newspaper Award in 1989.

Her first book, *Behind Closed Doors,* an exposé of the inequities in Canada's tax system, rocked the financial elite. In May 1991, she was awarded an Atkinson Fellowship for journalism in public policy. *The Quick and the Dead,* her second book, became a national bestseller.

# THE
# WEALTHY BANKER'S WIFE

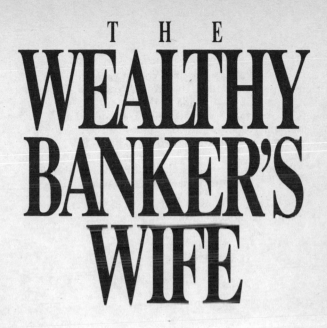

### THE ASSAULT ON EQUALITY IN CANADA

## LINDA McQUAIG

Penguin Books

PENGUIN BOOKS
Published by the Penguin Group
Penguin Books Canada Ltd, 10 Alcorn Avenue, Toronto, Ontario,
Canada M4V 3B2
Penguin Books Ltd, 27 Wrights Lane, London W8 5TZ, England
Penguin Books USA Inc., 375 Hudson Street, New York,
New York 10014, U.S.A.
Penguin Books Australia Ltd, Ringwood, Victoria, Australia
Penguin Books (NZ) Ltd, 182-190 Wairau Road,
Auckland 10, New Zealand

Penguin Books Ltd, Registered Offices:
Harmondsworth, Middlesex, England

First published 1993

1 3 5 7 9 10 8 6 4 2

Copyright © Linda McQuaig, 1993

Printed and bound in Canada

**Canadian Cataloguing in Publication Data**

McQuaig, Linda, 1951–
The wealthy banker's wife: the assault on equality in Canada

Includes bibliographical references.
ISBN 0-14-023065-3

I. Canada – Social policy.     I. Title.

HV108.M28 1993     361.6'1'0971     C93-093651-5

*To Peter, Donnie,*
*John and Wendy*
*who were great to grow up with*

# ACKNOWLEDGMENTS

I am very grateful to the Atkinson Charitable Foundation, *The Toronto Star* and the Beland Honderich family for jointly funding the research that went into this book, as part of a one-year journalism fellowship. There are few sources of funding for journalists who wish to investigate a subject in some depth, and I am therefore all the more appreciative of the opportunity offered by this fellowship.

Professor Abraham Rotstein of the Economics department at the University of Toronto provided crucial guidance in shaping the ideas and overall direction of the project. Adele Jushka, the fellowship's secretary, was always a pleasure to deal with. Kim Brooks and Linda Manzer both did a great job ferreting out research material.

Much of this research originally appeared in a series of articles in the *Star's* Insight section in November 1992, after considerable effort on the part of Chris Zelkovich, Lesly Taylor, John Ferri and Jim Atkins.

I also want to thank the hard-working crowd at Penguin Books — Cynthia Good, Brad Martin, Karen Cossar, Martin Gould, Barb Woodburne, Lori Ledingham, freelance copy editor Mary Adachi, and, of course, my delightful editor David Kilgour.

I am indebted as well to a number of individuals whose knowledge and insights helped me along the way: Tom Walkom, Linda Diebel, Mel Watkins, Leo Panitch, Ken Battle, Leon Muszynski and Daniel Drache. Jim Laxer was particularly generous with his time and ideas. As always, Neil Brooks was a key source of analytical help and inspiration.

It only remains to briefly thank my wonderful husband and ever-helpful editor, Fred Fedorsen.

# CONTENTS

# THE
# WEALTHY BANKER'S WIFE

# INTRODUCTION

Probably no other development in this century has affected the everyday lives of Canadians as much as the establishment of our social welfare programs. Prior to the Second World War, there was little security for Canadian families; an economic downturn or change in family circumstance could quickly bring disaster even to those whose lives had seemed safe and secure. The Depression of the '30s revealed just how vulnerable Canadians were, as middle-class families found themselves facing hunger and homelessness, or struggling to get by on meagre and degrading public relief. As part of a deliberate strategy of providing more financial security for Canadians, Ottawa over the years established unemployment insurance, pensions and family benefits so that circumstances beyond a family's control no longer automatically plunged it into poverty.

Furthermore, the introduction of universal programs in health care and education have dramatically altered our society, providing all Canadians —

regardless of income — with access to an education and to the most advanced medical care. These programs have created an unprecedented level of equality in two crucial areas of Canadian life.

And yet all this is now under attack.

We find ourselves confronted almost daily with news about yet more cuts in government spending, and more reductions in social services and benefits of all kinds — in the areas of health care, education, unemployment benefits, family benefits, pensions, welfare, community services, even programs for the disabled. Indeed, if we look at these cuts as a pattern, they make up what is perhaps the dominant theme of recent political developments in Canada — the move to restrain and cut back our social welfare systems, to move Canada towards a different model that relies less on government programs and more on the private marketplace. And, while social programs continue to be popular with Canadians, we have largely bought the message that all these cuts are necessary. For so long we have been inundated with stern warnings about the need to cut back our spending to maintain international competitiveness that many Canadians have reluctantly come to believe that we have no choice.

This book argues that we *do* have a choice. We have developed our way of thinking about this whole issue largely by focusing our sights on the United States, which has traditionally had a more limited social welfare system than we have and which in recent years has cut back even further its minimal social protections.

However, other nations, specifically those of western Europe, offer compelling alternatives. They are strong welfare states *and* they are economically competitive. Indeed, as I will argue in more detail later, there is no evidence that a strong welfare state interferes with economic growth and competitiveness. What a welfare state does do, however, is divide up a society's resources more equitably. And it is this — not the welfare state's alleged impact on economic growth — that has led to the attack on the welfare state by those unsympathetic to the egalitarian cause.

Few Canadians are even aware of the scope of the attack on our social systems. This is perhaps not surprising, because the attack has been carried out quietly and furtively. Certainly the Mulroney government never ran on a platform of social reform in either of its two national election campaigns. Indeed, as we all remember, it promised to preserve our universal social programs as a "sacred trust."

Yet the cuts introduced by the Mulroney government, in the form of complex and obscure budget changes, amount to truly massive spending reductions over time. The federal government's own advisory body, the National Council of Welfare, has projected that by the end of this decade, Ottawa will have reduced its spending on health and higher education by a total of $97.6 billion since 1986. Without ever announcing this intention, the federal government is quietly withdrawing from funding and overseeing these vital areas of our social welfare. Warns Michael Rachlis, a Toronto doctor and health policy analyst: "Unless the tide is reversed, medicare as Canadians have known it will be dead."

The attack has recently taken on a new dimension. Rather than just quietly cutting, the government — and others eager to see our social spending reduced — are now trying to get us to change the way we think about our social programs. Indeed, prominent people in government, business and the media seem to be trying to convince us that we're wrong to be so attached to these programs. Perhaps the best way to illustrate this is to use the example of medicare, the centrepiece of our social welfare system. Only a few years ago, politicians and commentators in Canada would no more question the value of medicare than their American counterparts would question the merit of maintaining a strong military arsenal. Just as military dominance had become a guiding principle in the American psyche, medicare had taken on a similar status in the minds and hearts of Canadians.

And yet it has now become acceptable — even fashionable in certain circles — to question the importance of medicare. At a recent public forum, one of the leading ministers in the Mulroney cabinet, Kim Campbell, noted that Canadians often mention medicare as one of the things they most value about their country. But, Campbell continued, medicare isn't enough to constitute a nation's identity or maintain a nation's pride.

Campbell seemed to be suggesting that medicare isn't as important as Canadians think — an odd comment for a federal cabinet minister to make about a national system that Canadians are proud of. Her willingness to challenge the importance of medicare was greeted with enthusiasm by William Thorsell, editor of *The Globe and Mail* and one of the leading voices of neoconservatism in Canada. Hailing her comments as "refreshing" in a column on the editorial page of his newspaper, Thorsell went on to question "the exalted status of medicare in our national psyche." Both Campbell and Thorsell seemed to be trying to tell Canadians to stop treating medicare like some national icon. But why?

Thorsell argued that our reverence for medicare "reflects the weakness of other conscious purposes in Canada." This echoes Campbell's assertion that medicare is insufficient to constitute a nation's identity or maintain its pride. What then would make a better source of national identity or pride? Surely when one compares medicare with the usual sources of national pride — a strong military force, foreign conquests, a successful sports team — medicare looks pretty impressive.

For Thorsell, medicare doesn't qualify as a source of national pride essentially because it's too soft. He lumps it in with other popular Canadian notions, like our role as international peacekeepers, low crime rates and multiculturalism, as evidence of our tradition of "caring," "compassion" and "social conscience." To

Thorsell, these traditions are apparently too mushy and weak to generate any real pride in Canada. Exactly what is inadequate about a tradition of caring, compassion and social conscience — as opposed to the usual nationalistic fare of militarism and bravado — is never explained.

In fact, medicare is much more than just a symbol of caring, compassion and conscience — all qualities that have to do with charity. If it was charity that Canadians took pride in, we would have elevated food banks to the status of national icon. But there is clearly little national pride in food banks.

There is, however, pride in medicare, as both Campbell and Thorsell acknowledge. And there's a reason for it. What medicare represents is an approach to society, an approach that *includes everyone*. Under this approach, we take a vital area of human life — health — and pool our collective resources as a society (through the tax system) to create an excellent system that provides an essential service to everyone. This is no small achievement. It reveals a commitment to more than charity; it reveals a commitment to equality, to a society where everyone is included, where everyone has rights to certain basic things. The benefits of this approach can be seen sharply against the counter example of a society which *excludes* certain segments of society. The United States, for instance, offers no universal health-care system to its citizens, and consequently access to proper medical care is often denied to those without sufficient financial resources.

Thorsell dismisses the lofty achievement of medicare by suggesting that it is somehow tied up with an alleged Canadian tendency to whine and complain and feel sorry for ourselves. "A nation of grieving souls is bound to value medicare," writes Thorsell. But why must we be seen as "grieving souls" for valuing a system that effectively deals with the health of the entire nation? What an achievement! I can think of few achievements that would make a better national icon.

As public figures and media commentators begin to question and even ridicule our reverence for medicare, their real purpose may be to undermine this inclusive approach to social welfare. Certainly, an approach that promotes inclusiveness and equality doesn't fit well with a new world order dominated by the ideology of international competitiveness, in which the sum total of human activity is the struggle to gain advantage over others. This is the world of the marketplace, and while the marketplace is an appropriate place for the trading of goods and services, it leaves much to be desired as the final arbiter of how we should run our country.

Regrettably, there appear to be many prominent people who would like to relegate the whole area of human well-being back to the marketplace, where it was before the rise of our social welfare systems. Much of this book deals with the disastrous consequences that this market approach has had south of the border.

The book grew out of a series of articles that I wrote for *The Toronto Star* in the fall of 1992, as part of a one-year Atkinson fellowship in public policy. The purpose of my research project was to examine the question of whether we could still afford the welfare state, given the new pressures of global competition. After dozens of interviews in Europe and North America, it became apparent to me that the United States and Europe have fundamentally different approaches to social welfare, that they represent two very different models.

The Europeans manage to maintain extensive social welfare systems and strong economies, while the Americans have convinced themselves that they can't afford anything more than the most minimal social programs. Canada, which has traditionally been situated somewhere between the two models, has recently been drifting in the American direction. Before we drift any further, we should remind ourselves that we do have a choice of directions, and that the direction we choose will ultimately determine what kind of society we live in.

Linda McQuaig
January 1993

# 1

## As Long as They Can Sell Their Blood...

In the long line of cabs parked in front of my Washington hotel, I selected the one that looked the most secure. The driver seemed delighted at my request for an hour-long tour, readily offering a special cut rate. Where did I want to go — the White House, Capitol Hill, Arlington Cemetery, the Lincoln Memorial? he asked. "Anacostia," I answered. His abrupt change of expression told me I might as well have said: "the moon."

In all his years as a cab driver in Washington, he said, no one had ever asked to be driven there — the sprawling black ghetto in the southeast corner of the U.S. capital on the other side of the Anacostia River. Although he was a large African-American, he said that he wouldn't answer a radio call for a pick-up there because he was afraid of what he might encounter. But he would make an exception so that a Canadian journalist could see the other half of the American dream. He rolled up the windows, locked all the doors and, in the broad daylight of high noon, we drove towards our fearsome destination. He shook his head: "We're just out here in the hands of the Lord."

As we crossed the river, we were quickly engulfed by the dreary remains of the once-viable working-class neighbourhood. There were abandoned cars and boarded-up houses and people with helpless, vacant looks. Driving deeper, the scenes grew grimmer. As we drove by block after block of dirty, low-rise housing projects, with walls smeared with graffiti and broken windows covered by wire mesh, I was struck by the realization that this descent into filth and degradation was happening in the richest country in the world, only minutes from the gleaming monuments to U.S. democracy.

When the state of Michigan eliminated welfare payments in October 1991, thousands of people were left with little choice but to sell their blood. "Selling blood is something that's always happened here," says Ted Phillips, executive director of the United Community Housing Coalition in Detroit. "But it was usually for something extra, like a security deposit for an apartment. Now people are driven to sell blood just to get by day to day."

Another desperation measure, Phillips says, is for poor people to sell their food stamp vouchers — for about 25 per cent of their value — in order to come up with the cash to pay for overnight accommodation in slum dwellings on cold winter nights. Then there's the growing number of homeless people who stand near the ramps of expressways with signs saying "Will work for food."

Michigan's cutback — which eliminated welfare payments for 90,000 adults, including 10,000 disabled people — has been repeated in various forms around the United States in an effort to reduce state budget deficits. Twelve states reduced their welfare payments for single adults, another thirteen cut back state benefits for poor families with children. The maximum monthly benefit in Mississippi for a mother and two children — *with no other source of income* — is now $120 (US).*

Far from the rubble of Anacostia and the blood-selling markets of the U.S. inner cities, Prime Minister Brian Mulroney addressed a different sort of crowd in a glittering Ottawa ballroom last November. It was a Conservative party fundraising dinner and the hundreds of guests were rich and extravagantly dressed. Each had paid $500 to attend which, incidentally, is more than three times the monthly benefit a Mississippi single mother gets to support herself and her children.

The slum dwellers of Anacostia and the dinner attendees in the Ottawa ballroom would recognize

---

* All dollar amounts used in this book are in Canadian dollars, unless otherwise indicated.

almost nothing from each others' worlds. Yet the Prime Minister would use the fundraising dinner to outline plans for Canada that could eventually make the world of Anacostia less remote to many Canadians unable to attend the gala event.

Mulroney told the Tory gathering that his government was planning to continue its crusade to reduce the federal deficit, indeed that it was planning further spending cuts. The government had paved the way for the Prime Minister's statement with the release two weeks earlier of a report by a federally appointed advisory committee stacked with business leaders and economists. The report, inappropriately titled *Inventing Our Future: An Action Plan for Canada's Prosperity*, called for major spending cuts to keep the deficit down.

The thrust of the Prime Minister's latest deficit-reduction campaign was in line with everything that the Mulroney government had done since coming to office in September 1984. But the renewed vigour of the campaign — in the midst of the worst recession since the '30s — was startling.

It was also a move that threatened to push Canada farther down the road to the kind of social breakdown that has happened in the United States. Although the U.S. has never had a strong social welfare system, its social safety net became considerably weaker in recent years, as both state and federal governments have slashed benefits in an attempt to control budget deficits. As usual, the poor have borne the brunt of the cutbacks and their anger and frustration were illustrated by the outpouring of rage in the Los Angeles riots last spring.

Canada has begun to move down this path too. Although Ottawa has treaded more cautiously, it has embarked on the same course of cutting social spending in the name of deficit reduction. Ironically, Ottawa seems determined to continue on this course, even as the U.S. may be about to loosen the federal purse strings. While it is too soon to tell what the new U.S. administration will do, President Bill Clinton at least campaigned on a platform that suggested a softening of the cut-and-slash approach to social spending that had characterized the Reagan-Bush years.

But the Conservative government has renewed and apparently deepened its commitment to cut spending. And, despite its unpopularity, it has largely succeeded in convincing Canadians that this is tough medicine, but medicine that must be taken. Indeed, while Canadians are wary about the potential impact of the cuts, we have been repeatedly told — to the point that many of us now believe it — that we simply have no choice.

We are told that we are living beyond our means, that we can no longer afford the generous social programs we developed in the prosperous postwar boom years. After almost a decade of lectures from business, government and the media about the need to cut government spending, many Canadians have become convinced that we must reduce our social programs if we want to compete in the global marketplace. "For

13

the past 16 years we have lived extensively beyond our means," warns the Canadian Manufacturers' Association in a 1990 brief calling on the federal government to cut social spending by $4.3 billion over five years. "We must cut our expenses to an affordable level. . . . Reality is that deficit reduction must be the top national priority."

Similar sentiments are constantly aired in the business press. "The cause of most concern is Canada's welfare state," said an editorial in the *Financial Post* in June 1991. "Two generations of Canadians have become spoiled, thanks to spendthrift politicians at all levels of government and with all parties . . . every politician from city councillors to cabinet ministers must cut programs and bureaucracies."

Influential business commentator William Mackness echoes the same theme. In an article in *The Globe and Mail's Report on Business Magazine* in April 1989, Mackness argued that "Canada's profligate social spending presents a tremendous moral hazard." Mackness, the chief economist at the Bank of Nova Scotia and former senior adviser in the office of then Finance Minister Michael Wilson, denounced Canada's "runaway social spending."

Some commentators go even farther to make their case. They tell Canadians that all this is essentially beyond our control, that we are powerless to resist the dictates of globalization. They tell us that this is all part of an inevitable future that is about to roll over us. To try to choose another course is to be a Luddite hopelessly trying to resist the march of history. Columnist Diane Francis for instance described free trade opponents in *Maclean's* as "latter-day King Canutes trying in vain to order an end to the tides." And economist Thomas Courchene, arguing for a revamping of Canada's social programs to make them more compatible with the private marketplace, insists that he is not being ideological, just recognizing the inevitable. He writes: "There is an underlying 'determinism' that will push the social policy system inexorably in these directions." Probably not since Lenin's heyday has there been such a tendency to believe that the world is in the grip of predetermined forces!

Indeed, the notion that our social spending is out of control has become so deeply ingrained in our current mindset that it goes virtually unchallenged. It is considered a fact, rather than a point of view.

But Canadians have developed this mindset largely by ignoring the massive evidence that contradicts it — namely, the example of the advanced countries of western and northern Europe. These countries, including Germany (for the purposes of this book, "Germany" refers to unified Germany or, before 1991, West Germany), France, Austria, Belgium, the Netherlands, Denmark, Sweden and Norway, spend far more on social programs than we do in North America — *and do as well or better than we do in economic growth and international competitiveness.*

These European nations spend a large percentage — between 18 and 30 per cent — of their Gross

Domestic Product on social security and other transfer payments, while Canada spends only 12.8 per cent, and the U.S. only 11.5 per cent.

**CHART 1 – Social Spending**
Government spending on social security and other transfers as a per cent of GDP, 1990.

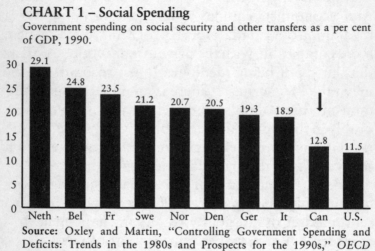

Source: Oxley and Martin, "Controlling Government Spending and Deficits: Trends in the 1980s and Prospects for the 1990s," *OECD Economic Studies*, No. 17, Table 2, Autumn 1991.

Yet these same European nations experienced economic growth that was as good as or better than ours in North America. With the exception of Norway, the European countries saw their productivity rise at a faster rate in the 1980s than either Canada or the United States.

Indeed, these European countries represent a compelling model — a model that challenges the conventional North American wisdom that large social welfare spending hampers economic growth. Contrary to the view that social spending is a drain

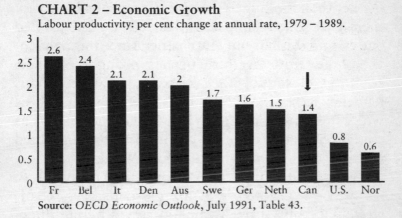

**CHART 2 – Economic Growth**
Labour productivity: per cent change at annual rate, 1979 – 1989.

Source: OECD *Economic Outlook*, July 1991, Table 43.

on the economy — and therefore something we must reduce in leaner times — the European countries show that high levels of social spending do not hinder economic growth. "If you look at growth rates, economic performance, productivity growth and compare it to trends [in social spending], you'll find there's no relationship — however you squeeze and twist the numbers," says Gosta Esping-Andersen, a professor of political and social science at the European University Institute in Florence, Italy.

Yet Canadians remain largely unfamiliar with the European model of social welfare. "We have a tendency here to not know about this other model," says Canadian political scientist James Laxer, author of *Inventing Europe*. This lack of knowledge is particularly odd, since Canadians share a similar level of economic development as well as a common cultural history with the advanced nations of Europe.

17

Rather than looking to Europe, Canadians have kept their gaze fixed almost exclusively on the United States, and this has only intensified since the Canada-U.S. Free Trade Agreement has brought our two countries closer together as trading partners. This tendency to see the U.S. as the only model has left us with a needlessly narrow view of the options. It has convinced us that the cost-cutting approach adopted by the U.S. is the only option for Canada.

This has vital implications for Canada's future. In many ways, Canada is at a crossroads. Two roads stretch in front of us, leading in very different directions. One road leads to a U.S.-style model of minimal social welfare; the other, to the more advanced social welfare models of western Europe.

If anything, Canada has been positioned roughly in the middle between the two poles. But in the past few years, we have been edging towards the U.S. model, although Ottawa has never come out and identified this as government policy. Before we move any closer to the U.S., we should be taking a hard look at the U.S. model — and the alternative model that Europe offers.

Certainly, observers on the other side of the Atlantic have a different way of looking at social welfare than do Americans. For Americans, social welfare is little more than a system of government hand-outs to the poor. The Europeans, on the other hand, view social welfare as a broad web of programs designed to ensure the well-being of the whole community. These programs are aimed at giving every member of the community access to health care, education and child care, as well as providing a reasonable amount of income maintenance for those who are elderly, sick, unemployed or taking care of young children. For the Europeans, there is a strong role for government in providing all this.

And while we in Canada tend to see the U.S. as the only model, the Europeans tend to regard the U.S., with its minimal social welfare programs, as something of an oddity. At the Paris-based Organization of Economic Co-operation and Development (OECD), the international body that closely monitors and analyses developments in the twenty-four leading industrial nations, analyst Edwin Bell describes the U.S. as unusual in the field of social welfare: "It is the outlier in this field, it is the most extreme."

The same idea is expressed more bluntly by American critics of the U.S. model. Larry Mishel, an economist at the Economic Policy Institute in Washington, describes the U.S. as the "dinosaur" of social welfare.

As we move closer to the "dinosaur," it seems to be increasingly difficult for us to see the more advanced species across the ocean, or to even keep in mind that there is a more advanced species. Consider, for instance, the following facts about the United States*

---

* This information is drawn from reports by the United Nations, the World Bank, the Luxembourg Income Study, etc. For more information on sources, see "References" at the end of the book.

— facts that paint a strikingly different portrait of American life than the Hollywood images we regularly see in American movies and television shows:

* Although the U.S. is among the richest countries in the world, it ranks among the worst in the industrialized world in just about any international measure of social standards.

* The gap between the rich and the poor is far more dramatic in the U.S. than in European countries.

* The U.S. poverty rate is two or three times as high as the poverty rates of the major European countries.

* The U.S. poverty rate for the most vulnerable group in society — children in single-parent families — is roughly ten times higher than in Sweden.

* The U.S. has a much worse record on infant mortality — a key measure of public health — than the major European countries; it ranks twenty-second in the world, behind even developing nations like Singapore.

* The U.S. ranks nineteenth in the world in the ratio of children to teachers in its schools, placing behind Libya, Lebanon and Cuba.

* More than seventy nations worldwide provide medical care to all pregnant women; the U.S., along with South Africa, does not.

* More than sixty nations provide medical care to all workers and their dependants; the U.S., along with South Africa, does not.

* Although the U.S. spends more per capita on health care than any country in the industrialized world, more than 35 million Americans have no health insurance coverage and an additional 40 million have such inadequate coverage that serious illness would lead to financial ruin.

* Black men in Harlem are less likely to reach the age of sixty-five than men in Bangladesh.

* More than one hundred nations provide paid maternity leaves for working mothers; the U.S. provides only unpaid maternity leave and many American women do not even qualify for unpaid leave.

* While the major European countries offer public day care for children three and over, the U.S. offers virtually no public day care.

* The notion of the U.S. as a land of opportunity is misleading; there is significantly *less* upward

21

mobility in the U.S. than in the major European countries.

Certainly, for Europeans, who have become accustomed to extensive social welfare programs, the U.S. model has little appeal. "They certainly do not want to go the way of the U.S.," says Dalmer Hoskins, secretary-general of the International Social Security Association, a Geneva-based international agency which monitors social security developments around the world.

Despite recession and harder economic times, there has been little pressure in Europe to cut back social welfare spending to the levels found in the U.S. The exception of course is Britain, where the Conservative government of Margaret Thatcher carried out an attack on the British welfare state that mirrored the neoconservative attacks of Ronald Reagan. But these neoconservative currents of Thatcher and Reagan have not undermined support for the welfare state in mainland Europe, according to George Ross, a sociologist at Brandeis University who specializes in European social policy. "The welfare state seems to be surviving rather well," notes Ross. "European electorates have so far demonstrated strong enough commitments to the welfare state to make European politicians pay attention."

Indeed, the familiar North American refrain that the welfare state is no longer affordable is rarely heard in Europe. "Why is it only in North America

— the two richest countries in the world — that people think they can't afford the welfare state?" asks Gosta Esping-Andersen, who specializes in international comparisons of welfare state policies.

Ironically, it is primarily nations that spend a relatively small percentage of their GDP on social welfare — like the United States and Canada — that are wringing their hands about the high costs of social programs, says Roger Beattie, an analyst with the International Labour Office, a Geneva-based affiliate of the United Nations. Beattie notes that in countries like France, Germany and the Netherlands, where social welfare spending is proportionately much higher, one rarely hears the view that the welfare state is no longer affordable, except from the extreme right. Even in Sweden, where the defeat of the Social Democrats in September 1991 led to speculation in North America about the demise of the welfare state, support for the welfare state remains strong — a subject to which we will return later.

Certainly the European results are impressive. "It's a tremendous success story; let's not overlook that," says Dalmer Hoskins, who was born in the U.S. "You can walk around European societies today and see the results. They have succeeded in most categories of social development as well as making strong economic progress. You don't have a situation here, as you do in the U.S., where people have simply fallen out of the system."

Only a short drive from Anacostia, the Heritage Foundation occupies a spacious medium-rise building near Capitol Hill. The foundation, a right-wing think-tank that has enjoyed enormous influence in U.S. political and media circles since the advent of Ronald Reagan and the new conservatism, is not terribly concerned about the poverty in U.S. ghettoes. Robert Rector, a young analyst at the foundation who is reputed to be influential with a number of congressmen, calls poverty a "bogus issue" which "takes attention away from the real issue — behavioural poverty." For Rector, the poor are poor because they're lazy.

A 1950s photograph reproduced in a Heritage Foundation pamphlet nicely captures the foundation's vision of America: a white middle-class family, smiling and well-dressed, sits around the dining-room table. The father, in a business suit, sits at the head of the table; his wife stands beside him, ready to serve the family dinner. For those at the Heritage Foundation, all that stands between the ghetto dwellers and this middle-class dream is, as Rector puts it, "lack of self-discipline."

In many ways, the most chilling aspect of the U.S. poverty problem is the fact that many Americans have become so desensitized to the poor that they no longer care whether a family of three can survive on $120 a month. After all, the poor can always sell their blood. For Canadians, this spectacle should make us pause before we dismantle our social welfare programs and make ourselves more like the "dinosaur."

# 2

# WHAT TO DO WITH THE
# WEALTHY BANKER'S WIFE?

Every month, the wife of the wealthy bank president delighted as she opened the envelope from Ottawa and found a cheque for $34. Now, how would she spend this little gift from the government? What would it be this time — imported bath oils, a box of chocolates, a new cologne?

Never mind that this image of the wealthy banker's wife and her monthly family allowance cheque was largely a myth. (Few, if any, bank presidents' wives had children young enough to qualify for the monthly payments.) What mattered was the image. And the image that was bandied about in the media was that of a wealthy family receiving a government cheque each month — while the federal deficit was careering wildly out of control. It seemed like the perfect example of government spending gone haywire.

So there were few protests in February 1992 when Ottawa announced that it was finally cancelling the family allowance program, which for more than four decades had been available to all families with young children. Instead, the Mulroney government said it would target the money more directly at the poor. While there were no tears shed behind the wrought-iron gates of the Rosedale mansions — or wherever bank presidents and their wives live — the cancellation of the family allowance program had far-reaching implications for Canada.

How could a measly $34 a month have far-reaching implications for Canada? It's true that $34 today would barely pay for a month's supply of diapers. But this is because the federal government allowed the value of the family allowance payments to be badly eroded over the years. When the program was established in 1945, it was a generous program — available to all families — and a key income support for millions of those families, according to Brigitte Kitchen, a professor of social work at York University in Toronto.

Indeed, a family with three children received family allowance payments that in 1945 amounted to 20 per cent of the average industrial wage. This meant that, for couples with three or more children, the family allowance cheque was enough to pay the monthly rent or grocery bill for the whole family. It was thus a significant part of the family's income — and deliberately so. The federal government had set the levels high as part of a strategy of income support to keep families from slipping into poverty. If there was one lesson that Canadians had learned from the bitter days of the Depression of the '30s, it was the vulnerability of all Canadians — particularly those with children — to the swings of the economy. What Canadians wanted was a system that would protect them from the arbitrary dictates of the marketplace.

But they didn't want to be dependent on public relief, or what we now call "welfare." The Depression had left hundreds of thousands of previously self-sufficient Canadians dependent on public relief, and it had been a humiliating experience that left a strong and lasting impression. When the war was finally over, and Canadians returned home, what they wanted were jobs and a system that would give their families some real security — and prevent them from being turned into paupers on public relief when the economy turned bad again.

The vision of a more secure life for Canadians in the postwar era was reflected in the recommendations of the *Report on Social Security for Canada*, which the federal government commissioned academic Leonard Marsh to write in the early '40s.

Marsh urged the government to keep people off public relief by committing itself to full employment, and to ongoing income security for families. The backbone of this more secure system would be a family allowance program, a system of unemployment insurance benefits and old-age pensions. The government followed through with a universal family allowance program immediately after the war and a universal old-age pension in 1951. (An unemployment insurance system had been introduced in 1940.)

27

At the outset, the family allowance program in Canada was generous, following the example of European countries like France and Sweden that already had such programs to support all families. Germany, which had been devastated by the war, quickly followed with a family allowance program as well. But while the European countries have largely kept up their programs over the years, Canada allowed its program to decline in value, until it was finally axed by the Mulroney government. The European programs vary from country to country, but they generally amount to a sizeable payment — roughly 5 to 10 per cent of the median wage. (In Canadian terms, that would amount to roughly $90 to $180 a month per child.) Particularly in larger families, the payments can continue to be an important source of family income in Europe.

The Mulroney government's decision to cancel the family allowance program has pushed us farther from the European model of social welfare towards a U.S.-style social welfare system.

To understand the significance of this it is necessary to consider briefly the difference between the two models. Of course, the models are not totally distinct; there are similar aspects in both. But it is not over-simplifying to say that they represent two different approaches based on two different notions of how society should function.

In the U.S.-style model, the well-being of the citizenry is largely left up to the private marketplace.

This approach is rooted in the notion that people function best under the discipline of the market, where the need to survive drives them to work hard. The role of the state should be limited, since most members of society will prosper when left to their own devices. The state should only intervene where it is necessary to protect those who are simply too weak or too vulnerable to make it on their own.

The European model, on the other hand, sees society as more than just an adjunct of the private marketplace. In fact, it regards the marketplace with some suspicion, seeing it as an imperfect mechanism that generates tremendous inequalities. Society must therefore limit the power of the private market in certain areas, in the interests of ensuring the well-being of the whole community.

The difference between these two approaches can best be seen in the different attitudes the Americans and the Europeans have towards the concept of "welfare." To the Americans, it is a last-resort payment made to those who are too weak to survive on their own. To the Europeans, however, the concept of welfare is linked to the broader concept of "social welfare," and implies a set of social rights and responsibilities. What matters is not just the well-being of the individual, but the well-being of all members of society. Society is seen as an interconnected community where everyone contributes to the communal purse and everyone benefits from it. In this sense, everyone is part of the welfare state.

This may explain why the word "welfare" has a highly negative connotation in the United States, but a positive connotation in Europe, notes Edwin Bell, from the OECD. In the European model, the welfare state involves more than just hand-outs to the poor. Rather it encompasses all areas of well-being — health care, education, child care, pensions and protection against loss of income — and benefits in these areas are generally available to everyone.

In Scandinavia, where the universal social welfare model is most advanced, special means-tested programs directed exclusively at the poor have been all but eliminated. The Social Democrats who designed the Swedish welfare state in the '30s specifically sought to avoid targeting benefits exclusively to the poor — something that was associated with the Poor Law, the hated eighteenth-century law which provided minimal assistance to the destitute. "The Social Democrats' most pressing social policy aim was thus the creation of a system of social insurance which gave a real sense of security to the citizens of the country," notes Walter Korpi, professor of social policy at the Swedish Institute for Social Research in Stockholm. "The system they strove to achieve would ensure security against hardship in the case of accident, illness, unemployment and in old age."

We can see the difference between the European and U.S. model vividly if we return to the example of family allowances. The European countries offer a family allowance to all families; in the Netherlands, even the

Queen received it when her children were young! The principle behind this "universal" approach is that raising children is more than just the responsibility of individual parents. Rather, it is, to some extent, the responsibility of the whole community. Society therefore should shoulder part of the costs.

In the U.S., however, the individual family is on its own, and raising children is viewed as an individual responsibility. The state generally only intervenes to help in cases of need by, for instance, providing food stamps to poor families to cash in at supermarkets.

It is easy to see how the European model — and the model adopted by Canada right after the war — creates a more cohesive community, with less of a stigma attached to being from a low-income family. Cashing a family allowance cheque is something that everyone does, something that all are entitled to, as a result of living and working and paying taxes in the country. By contrast, the food stamp recipient is outside the mainstream, cashing in a benefit provided by others, so that his or her family doesn't have to beg on the street for food. It puts the family on the public dole — the fate that Canadians right after the war were determined to avoid.

The European system is more intrinsically appealing. There is something awful about a system that leaves parents feeling that they are unable to provide for their children as other parents do, that they are reliant on special aid packages which go only to the poor. Still, aesthetics aside, the more important issue

31

is: which system works better to help those most in need?

The "targeted" approach used by the U.S. may seem sensible at first glance, particularly in situations where there are pressures on government to restrain spending. Rather than squandering funds on the middle and upper classes — like the wealthy banker's wife or, for that matter, the Queen — the targeted approach directs resources specifically to the needy. This presumably frees up extra resources for the poor. Similarly, we might expect that the interests of the poor would somehow get lost, or at least not get the attention they deserve, in the universal systems found in Europe.

Yet the truth is exactly the opposite — and dramatically so. The Americans have an absolutely dismal record in helping the poor, while the Europeans have done much better, and the Scandinavians — where the universal social welfare model has been applied most comprehensively — have the best record of all.

The Americans have been surprisingly ungenerous with the poor. Despite claims that they are targeting the poor specifically, and presumably with extra cash saved by not providing payments to all families, benefit levels in the U.S. still keep families well below the poverty line. A recent report prepared by the Center on Budget and Policy Priorities in Washington found appallingly low benefit levels.

The levels fluctuate across the country, since they are set by individual state governments, with joint funding from federal and state coffers. But the pattern is clear: benefits are low. In a relatively generous state, such as New York, a family of three with no other source of income was entitled to a maximum benefit of $577 (US) a month in 1992. In a less generous state, such as Idaho, the same family had to live on $317 (US). In one of the least generous states, such as Alabama, the family of three somehow had to figure out how to get by on $149 (US) a month. (There were five states with benefits under $200 [US] a month, including Mississippi, mentioned in the last chapter, where a family of three was limited to a monthly payment of $120[US]) Even when the value of food stamps was added in, the report found that families were still well below the poverty line.

Benefits in the U.S. have in fact been declining over the past two decades. Data compiled by the U.S. Congressional Research Service show that between 1970 and 1991 benefits declined in a typical state by 42 per cent, after adjusting for inflation. Thus, the benefits received in 1991 were on average worth $265 (US) a month less — or about $3,000 (US) a year less — than what would have been available to them two decades earlier.

Poor people without children found it even more difficult to get benefits. Twenty-two states provided no benefits at all to poor individuals without children; some local communities provided benefits in these cases, but many did not, the report found.

So, despite an apparent effort to target benefits to the

poor, the U.S. has a particularly bad record in helping the poor. The U.S. poverty rate among the non-elderly population is 18.1 per cent — roughly double the poverty rate of the major European countries, according to the Luxembourg Income Study, an internationally recognized income data base that uses a standard measure to compare incomes in different countries. Germany, by comparison, has a poverty rate of 6.8 per cent, France 9.9 per cent, Sweden 8.6 per cent.

**CHART 3 – Poverty**
Poverty rates in selected countries.

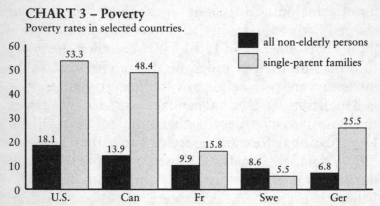

**Source:** Timothy Smeeding and Lee Rainwater, "Gross-National Trends in Income Poverty and Dependency." Joint Center for Political and Economic Studies, Washington, D.C., 1991. Based on data from the Luxembourg Income Study.

The differences become more pronounced, however, in cases involving particularly vulnerable members of society — such as children with only one parent. Although this is the group targeted by the biggest welfare program in the U.S., Aid to Families with

Dependent Children, poverty among these children shoots up to an astonishing 53.3 per cent in the U.S., compared to Germany with 25.5 per cent, France with 15.8 per cent and Sweden with only 5.5 per cent.

Members of the U.S. Congress were shocked in September 1991 when Timothy Smeeding, director of the Luxembourg Income Study, presented data comparing the U.S. and European poverty rates. After outlining the dismal U.S. performance, Smeeding, a U.S. economist, was blunt. The United States, he said, tolerates "a level of disadvantage unknown to any other major country on earth."

The reason targeted programs don't work, according to many analysts, is that it is difficult to maintain political support among the population for programs that only benefit a small portion of society. On the other hand, if taxpayers feel that a program offers important benefits for themselves and their family members, they are much more willing to support it — even pay high taxes to maintain it. "It is difficult for many people to conceive that tax levels in excess of 50 per cent of Gross Domestic Product, as they are in Sweden, are tolerable," says Leon Muszynski. "But they can be tolerable if the majority of people benefit by the social security it provides."

In countries like Sweden the welfare state provides significant benefits for just about everyone. A senior executive in a private company is well aware of the benefits; his wife may well be employed in a job in the social welfare bureaucracy while his children attend high-quality public day care and the family enjoys a seven-week holiday each year, which is fairly common in Sweden.

Interestingly, the best evidence of the wide base of support for universal programs may come from the U.S.

The U.S., as we have seen, has generally designed its social programs to target the poor, rather than providing benefits for all citizens. The exception to this, however, are programs for the elderly. The old-age pension is universal in the U.S., and there is free medical care for all seniors. As a result, these programs enjoy a huge constituency of support, and have been almost invulnerable to attempts by politicians to reduce spending. The Reagan administration — at the height of its popularity — proposed significant cuts to old-age security in 1981, only to be greeted by a huge public outcry and a sharp rebuff from Congress. Apparently, few politicians were willing to risk tampering with a program that so many Americans relied on for themselves and their family members.

Indeed, the effective political fight waged by U.S. seniors reveals the potential for popular mobilization in support of universal programs, even in the context of a *laissez-faire* political climate like the U.S. As Canadian academic John Myles has noted, a coalition of seniors groups called Save Our Security blossomed into a massive national movement with more than 35 million members in response to Reagan's proposed cuts. Another national group, formed in 1982 to lobby to preserve pensions and free medical care for the elderly, quickly attracted 5 million members. And the largest of the groups representing the elderly, the American Association of Retired Persons, now claims 28 million members, a paid staff of 1,300, an annual budget of more than $200 (US) million and a monthly magazine, *Modern Maturity*, with one of the highest circulations in the United States.

The ambivalence of taxpayers towards programs they don't benefit from, on the other hand, can also be seen in the U.S. There was considerable hostility on the part of many middle- and upper-income taxpayers to the Catastrophic Health Care Bill of 1988. The bill would have imposed a special surtax to pay for a program to help families deal with the costs of enormous medical bills. Resistance to the bill came largely from those who were already covered for medical disasters through private insurance plans, and resented having to pay a surtax to help others who didn't have such insurance.

"There must be a lesson there," says Dalmer Hoskins, from the International Social Security Association in Geneva. "There seems to be broad-based support for systems where there's a conviction on the part of the people who are paying that they are getting something out of it. It's not considered a fair deal if people pay and the benefits all go to others."

Oddly enough, all the complaints about benefits

going to the wealthy banker's wife were coming from people like the wealthy banker.

The wealthy banker's wife was, of course, little more than a symbol — a symbol for the notion that universal social programs squander public resources needlessly on the rich. But what is striking about the debate over "universality" is the way the complaints about this supposed boondoggle for the rich have come largely from the rich and those who represent the rich. It has been Conservatives — not New Democrats or the labour movement — who have led the charge to strip the proverbial wealthy banker's wife of her benefits, and there has been a chorus of support from the business press.

Indeed, the wealthy banker and his wife have become a favourite whipping boy for the Conservatives. When the Mulroney government tried to cut back old-age pensions in May 1985, it justified its move by suggesting that it was absurd for government pension benefits to go to retired bank presidents.

But while the wealthy banker seems to have taken quite a beating in government and business rhetoric, one fact quickly emerges: he has not taken a beating in real life. The Conservative government has been anything but hard on the banks or their presidents. Much of the Mulroney government's agenda has been to put in place policies favoured by the banks: free trade, deficit reduction, high interest rates. Indeed, if we try to think of what groups have fared well under the Tories, it would be hard to imagine bankers not being prominent on a very short list. And, as high-income Canadians, bankers have benefited from the Conservative government's drop in the top income tax rate, more generous RRSP deductions and the special exemption for capital gains.

So it is odd, to say the least, to find the Conservatives so willing to pick on the hapless banker when it comes to social programs. Perhaps the answer to this perplexing riddle is that cancelling social benefits for the rich does nothing to hurt the rich. The bank president and his wife don't really mind giving up their family allowance cheque and their old-age pensions. After all, they don't need the extra cash to raise a family and they no doubt have ample private retirement plans and personal savings. Nor, for that matter, do they need a good unemployment insurance or welfare system. These public programs, while terribly important to millions of Canadians, are virtually irrelevant to the lives of the rich. Even our premier social programs — public education and medicare — mean far less to the rich, who often prefer to send their children to private schools anyway and would be just as happy to pay extra fees for more exclusive medical care.

But if the rich are not terribly concerned about the benefits of our social programs, there is one thing that concerns them a great deal — the cost of providing these programs to others. High-level social programs are costly to maintain, and ultimately must be paid for with taxes. All Canadians of course pay taxes, but most Canadians receive vital social benefits in exchange. The rich, however, pay taxes and receive social benefits they don't particularly care about. In a sense, they are paying taxes to support programs that primarily benefit others. It is easy to see why the rich often come to believe they would be better off if every family simply took care of itself.

This points to a crucial aspect of the social welfare state — that it is more important to some than to others. This is because what the welfare state does, above all, is reduce inequalities in our society.

Left to its own devices, the private marketplace distributes income in a highly unequal manner, creating great concentrations of wealth at the top and poverty at the bottom. Social programs can even out some of these disparities, largely by making payments that help prop up those at the lower end. We can see this clearly if we look at Statistics Canada data showing the percentage of income received by different segments of the population before and after social payments. Before social payments, the poorest 20 per cent of Canadians received only 1.2 per cent of all income in 1989. After social payments, however, the families in this bottom group increased their share of total income to 4.8 per cent — still obviously a very small share of the national pie, but a significant improvement over the share distributed to them by the private marketplace.

If we continue up the income ladder we see that the

equalizing effect of social programs continues. Looking at the next 20 per cent of Canadian families (that is, the second poorest group), we see that they also enjoyed a significant increase in their share of the national income as a result of social payments. The middle 20 per cent stayed about the same, with the 20 per cent right above them receiving a somewhat smaller share. When we reach the top 20 per cent, we see that after social payments are made this richest group of Canadians has a smaller overall share of the national income — 43.2 per cent, as opposed to the 47.2 per cent allocated to them by the private marketplace.

In case this sounds like quibbling over small differences, it should be noted that small differences in percentage points amount to large amounts of money. For example, if the government had not intervened with social payments but had simply left the market to its own devices, the bottom 20 per cent of Canadians would have had *$15.7 billion less income!* To get a clearer picture of the impact of this on people's lives, we can figure out how much additional income this provided to each of the two million households* that make up the poorest 20 per cent of Canadians. Before social payments, each of these two million households had an average annual income of just $2,189 — a meagre amount that would clearly not be enough to

---

*"Household" refers to families of all sizes, as well as to unattached individuals.

feed the members of the household, not to mention providing shelter and clothing. After social payments are added, however, the average household income for the two million poorest households rose to $9,860 — an increase of $7,671.

Another way to to illustrate the impact of the welfare state on equality is to show how much more low-income Canadians depend on social transfer payments they receive from government. As we've just seen, the incomes of the bottom group of Canadians rose on average by $7,671 as a result of social payments. However, social payments boosted the incomes of the top group of Canadians on average by only $2,650.

The role of the social welfare system as a vehicle for redistribution is particularly important since it is really the only vehicle for redistribution. The tax system could perform such a function, and indeed it appears to, by applying higher marginal tax rates to those in higher income brackets. But the truth is that the Mulroney government has flattened the tax rates and generally overhauled the tax system in a way that has eased the burden on the rich. Neil Brooks, a tax professor at Osgoode Hall Law School in Toronto, notes that Canada's tax system now has little impact on the distribution of income. He says that social programs do considerably more to redistribute resources from the rich to the poor and middle class.

But the picture painted by statistics doesn't tell the full story of how our social welfare system creates a more equal society. The statistics don't, for instance, include the impact of social services such as public education and medicare. Without these public systems, which make high-level education and medical care available to all Canadians, there would be far greater disparities between the lives of the rich and the poor. Indeed, if it weren't for medicare and public education, these two crucial areas of human development would be handed over to the private marketplace, and the quality of service would depend on the financial resources of the customer. Canadians without financial resources would inevitably end up with poorer education and less medical care.

So it is perhaps not surprising that the people calling for an end to our universal systems are those who benefit least from a reduction in inequality — people like the wealthy banker and his wife. In fact, it could be said that these sorts of people are comfortable with inequality — an inequality where they are among the privileged few.

In many ways, demands for government spending cuts attack the very egalitarian goals of the welfare state. For decades after the Second World War, the welfare state expanded, creating programs that made real and important differences in the lives of ordinary people. As long as the economy was booming, as it was in the early postwar years, the growth of the welfare state was more or less accepted by all groups in society. But with the economic slowdown that has plagued the West since the mid-'70s, that consensus has fallen apart. Suddenly, the high cost of social welfare programs seems exorbitant — especially to those who don't particularly need them. The neoconservative philosophy ushered in by Ronald Reagan and Margaret Thatcher is really a political reaction against the welfare state and its egalitarian goals.

Of course, neoconservatives have many arguments against the welfare state. They argue, for instance, that the welfare state produces inefficiencies and stagnates economic growth through high government spending. But, as we've already seen, there is really no evidence that high government spending reduces economic growth — a subject to which we will return later. What the welfare system *does* do, however, is reduce inequality. It by no means eliminates it, but it redistributes income in a slightly fairer way and it creates public systems that give all members of society access to crucial public services.

The attack on our social welfare system by neoconservatives is really an attack on equality. They want us to rely more on the private marketplace to make decisions, including decisions about how resources are divided up among the country's residents. The fact that the marketplace produces large disparities between the rich and the poor is not something that concerns neoconservatives, who generally tend to be on the richer end of the spectrum. Reaganomics was really little more than a philosophy of pandering to the rich, based on the argument that the rich held the key to prosperity. Only by increasing the holdings of the rich, it said, could we hope to generate an economic boom that would eventually (someday) trickle down to everyone else. It is easy to see why this sort of thinking found considerable support among the rich.

Neoconservatism has made it once again fashionable to be rich. The media pay lavish attention to the lifestyles of the rich, and books extol the remarkable achievements of businessmen who only a decade or so ago would have been seen in a less flattering light as greedy corporate tycoons. The idea of a progressive tax system — where the rich pay proportionately more than others — is increasingly frowned upon. It is said to destroy incentives and to be an unfair seizure of the private property of the rich, who will simply leave the country if the tax bill grows too big. James Laxer captures the essence of neoconservatism when he describes it as "the reassertion of the legitimacy of inequality." Whereas the welfare state argued for greater equality, neoconservatism makes a case for *in*equality. There's nothing wrong with being rich, it says; the rich are rich because they contribute more to society, not because they've managed to horde the lion's share for themselves.

Indeed, some neoconservatives, like Canadian writer William Gairdner, actively push for inequality. Gairdner is an avowed opponent of the welfare state, and his arguments against it are revealing. He opposes the welfare state largely because it strives to achieve greater equality — which Gairdner sees as a wrong-headed goal. To Gairdner, people are intrinsically unequal — some run faster than others, for instance — and the state should not intervene to correct the imbalances that result from these natural inequalities. Indeed, Gairdner goes so far as to argue that the state should intervene to *preserve* these inequalities. In his recent book, *The War Against the Family*, Gairdner writes: "The State and its courts must protect and nourish such natural inequalities because they are the signal guarantor of a free society."

The free society Gairdner has in mind is indeed free for the powerful private interests who would basically run it. Gairdner would like to see a drastically reduced role for government, and a much stronger reliance on the private marketplace — a nice formula for those who are pleased with the way the marketplace distributes resources. Gairdner himself has reason to be pleased. He was born into a wealthy family. When he advocates privatizing our public schools and criticizes our system of "socialized medicine," we know that he and his family would in no way be harmed by the breakdown of these public systems. Gairdner can no doubt buy his family all the private health care and education they would want. It is the rest of the Canadian population that would suffer.

To get a glimpse of what that suffering might be, we don't have far to look.

# 3

# FREEDOM TO DIE: SOCIAL WELFARE IN THE U.S.A.

The fact that some 35 million Americans have no health insurance is startling enough. What is perhaps more startling is the explanation. One might expect defenders of the U.S. system to argue that a national public health insurance scheme is simply too expensive. Instead, it turns out, the explanation has something to do with "freedom."

One such defender, Mark V. Pauly, says that people who don't buy private health insurance may simply be "individuals who truly are risk-loving, who derive pleasure from playing in the high-stakes lottery that might leave them financially wiped out if serious illness strikes."

In case one is tempted to dismiss Mark V. Pauly as simply a flake, it should be noted that he occupies some fairly senior academic posts: he is chairman and professor of the Health Care Systems Department and professor of insurance, public policy and management at the Wharton School, and a professor of economics at the University of Pennsylvania. Furthermore, he has served as executive director of the Leonard Davis Institute of Health Economics. In short, Pauly's comments pass for serious commentary in the U.S. on health-care issues.

So let's look a little closer at what he has to say about those who don't buy private health insurance. Pauly even has a term for these reckless characters: "the Evel Knievels of health-care costs." But he argues — in all seriousness — that it is important to defend their right to choose to go without health insurance! "There is a fundamental issue here: the freedom of individuals to engage in behaviour that their fellow citizens regard as unattractive or even irresponsible," writes Pauly in a special health-care report put out last year by the right-wing American Enterprise Institute. Freedom in America, it seems, includes the freedom to be without health insurance.

Pauly's use of the concept of "freedom" may seem bizarre to those outside the United States. Most Europeans — and Canadians — would be more concerned about the freedom to have access to health care than the freedom to be denied it. But Pauly's argument in many ways explains how the American obsession with the private marketplace — an obsession that pervades the U.S. approach to social welfare — has left it with social standards that are among the lowest in the Western world.

In the U.S. view, the market is deemed to function effectively. So if millions of people are without health insurance, they are presumably doing so out of choice — just as they might choose not to buy a new sofa for the living room. In this view, social welfare is not a right of citizenship but rather a consumer item. Indeed, health care in the U.S. is like other commercial areas, with some 1,500 private insurance companies competing for the business of consumers, offering what amounts to boutique shopping; consumers can now purchase specialized disease packages, such as coverage for a particular type of cancer.

This emphasis on the private market in social benefits has important effects. Most importantly, it means that vast numbers of people simply go without benefits. And, despite theories about the "Evel Knievels of health-care costs," the truth is that millions of Americans lack health coverage not because they enjoy the thrill of living without it, but because they simply can't afford it. (Adequate coverage starts at about $5,000 [US] a year for a family of four — well out of the range of most U.S. families. And even with this insurance, customers still face a $600 deductible on all health bills, including doctors' visits. As a result, typical out-of-pocket expenses for the family of four per year are in the range of $2,000 — over and above the $5,000 cost of premiums.)

The U.S. provides free health-care coverage for some — although by no means all — of the poor. But even the poor who qualify for free coverage can have difficulty gaining access to proper care, since the majority of physicians do not accept patients on the government plan because the fees are too low. Elderly Americans also receive free health-care coverage under a government plan, but the payment rates are so low that many doctors charge extra fees. As a result, elderly patients end up buying additional medical insurance, and still face large deductibles. For those who have no coverage, there are overcrowded public hospitals where patients face long line-ups and often undesirable conditions. Even at these public hospitals, payment is demanded up front. Those without funds are eventually treated but often hounded later by collection agencies. As a result, many without coverage do not seek treatment until their condition has become acute.

It is interesting to see how supporters of the U.S. free market approach perform intellectual somersaults to avoid dealing with the issue of affordability. Pauly, for instance, never directly refers to the problem that some people might lack the extra $7,000 a year to pay for health-care coverage. Instead, he characterizes their lack of insurance as a "choice." He suggests that "ideal levels of care are diverse because citizens have diverse preferences." In other words, some people buy a lot of medical insurance simply because they happen to like having access to medical care, whereas other people would just as soon not have medical care — for themselves and their loved ones. It's all just what turns you on.

The closest Pauly comes to acknowledging the financial factor is when he recommends a system that would require everyone to purchase the minimum private insurance that "a 'reasonable' person at each income level" would buy. This would presumably provide everyone with the insurance — and the level of medical care — that is "appropriate" for someone in his or her income bracket. One can imagine how this system would work: a rich person with heart disease would benefit from all the latest treatments, an upper-middle-class person would perhaps receive most of the latest treatments, an ordinary middle-class person would receive some treatments but not too many, a lower-middle-class person might be wise to find himself a good faith healer, and so on.

Unfortunately this kind of indifference to people at the lower end is not confined to the U.S. Some Canadian academics too have weighed in with support for the market approach to health care, and have attempted to undermine the confidence of Canadians in their public system. Prominent among them is University of Toronto historian and media personality Michael Bliss, who reveals a taste for the U.S. health-care system in a column in *The Globe and Mail's Report on Business Magazine* in September 1991. Bliss takes comfort from a U.S. academic report by Henry J. Aaron of the Brookings Institution that, according to Bliss, showed the U.S. health-care situation is not "nearly as bleak as we like to think." Bliss continues cheerfully: "Most of the 30 million or so 'uninsured' Americans are only temporarily without coverage and many of these are from healthy segments of the population."

So it seems we shouldn't be too worried about the more than 30 million Americans — including 10 million children — without health coverage. After all, Bliss assures us, many of them come from healthy segments of the population. (And what about the ones who don't?) No doubt Bliss would be content to be without health insurance for himself and his family, as long as they were all currently healthy, or at least belonged to "healthy segments of the population." Healthy people, as we all know, never require medical care — they never have car accidents or need their appendix out or have babies or develop cancer.

Furthermore, the plight of the uninsured is only temporary, Bliss says. But this situation is more serious than Bliss would have us believe. Americans are often without coverage because they have lost their jobs, and thus their job-related health benefits, or because their employer has cancelled a health plan and they can't afford the premiums on their own. As Henry Aaron himself points out in his report: "The number who have no insurance at all on any one date understates the risk of being uninsured." Essentially, anyone whose health insurance is connected to work, which is common in the U.S., risks being uninsured at some time. Writes Aaron: "By this criterion, more than 60 million Americans are at risk of losing insurance."

The benign view of defects in the U.S. health-care system expressed by Bliss and Pauly do not square with the more damning accounts of the system found just about everywhere outside the writings of the neo-conservative right. In a massive overview of health-care systems within industrialized nations, a 1990 OECD report presents the U.S. in a most unflattering international perspective. In a lead article in the report, Alain C. Enthoven, professor of management and health economics at Stanford University, writes: "What can Europeans learn from Americans about the financing and organization of medicare care? The obvious answer is: 'not much.' We Americans are spending nearly 12 per cent, going on 15 per cent, of gross national product (GNP) on health care, while most European countries are spending an apparently stabilized 6 to 9 per cent. . . . The western European democracies have achieved essentially universal coverage, but some 35 million Americans — 17.5 per cent of the population under 65 years of age — have no financial protection against medical expenses, public or private. . . . Millions more have inadequate coverage that leaves them exposed to large risks or to exclusions for care of preexisting conditions. At the same time, our infant mortality rate is higher than that of most of the western European democracies. . . . I could go on. We have much to be humble about."

Vicente Navarro, professor of health policy and sociology at Johns Hopkins University in Baltimore, estimates that roughly one hundred thousand people die each year in the U.S. because they cannot pay for needed medical care, and most of these victims are low-income workers and their families. Comments Navarro: "The pain and suffering for millions of workers and their families is excruciating. Imagine for a moment having your loved ones sick and not being able to do anything about it because you cannot afford medical care. For millions and millions, this is the daily reality in their lives."

Even Henry Aaron, whom Bliss cites as providing a brighter view of the U.S. system, is in fact highly critical of it and its failure to provide coverage for so many Americans. Aaron's report notes that the proportion of Americans without health insurance is higher than a decade ago, that lack of coverage is closely connected to lack of financial resources, and that the net impact appears to be poorer health results for the millions of uninsured Americans. Aaron cites a study from the *Journal of the American Medical Association* showing that "lack of insurance makes a significant difference in therapy and in outcomes of treatment." Concludes Aaron: "The idea that the seriously ill receive standard therapy whether or not they have insurance seems to be a comforting delusion."

Bliss, however, is more concerned about the line-ups in the Canadian health-care system, although he provides no evidence that this is a serious problem. A more thoughtful commentator, Dr. Michael Rachlis, a Toronto health-care consultant and epidemiologist, comments: "While there are waiting lists for some elective procedures, emergency cases are dealt with immediately. Patients are prioritized by need, not by bank balance."

Like Pauly, Bliss deftly skirts around the touchy issue of affordability in a private health-care system. His main concern appears to be that the Canadian system limits the rights of people who could afford to spend even more on health care, presumably to put themselves at the front of the line of those waiting for elective surgery. Thus he complains that the Canadian health-care system takes away "your freedom to buy better or faster health-care service" and, as a result, "[d]ogs will continue to have better access to health care in Canada than people," because there's no limit on how much a rich person can pay to have his dog treated.

No doubt there are some Canadians who are rich enough to build a private hospital for their dog and hire the finest surgeons in the world to staff it! But is this relevant to a debate about how to best spend our health-care dollars to ensure the health of Canadian people? For Bliss, the fact that the Canadian system limits the rights of the rich to buy their way to the front of the line is more troubling than the fact that the U.S. health-care system leaves more than 35 million Americans without any guarantee of care at all.

In the full-page, glossy magazine advertisement, the white face of a successful businessman stands out among a group of mostly young blacks and Hispanics. They all stand together smiling in a classroom setting, in front of a backdrop of math equations, school announcements and a poster with the words: "I'll be a success." The businessman is identified as the CEO of ARCO, "the high energy company" which funds educational programs in schools like this one in East Los Angeles.

The ad is more than just good public relations for ARCO. It is part of a movement in the U.S. that sees a key role for business in rescuing the U.S. education system.

After more than a decade of drastic cuts in spending on schools, the U.S. public school system is in terrible shape. And for businessmen and others, this represents an opportunity. A "growing bunch of entrepreneurs," reported *The New York Times* in a 1991 education supplement, "are suggesting that unabashed capitalism can succeed . . . where bureaucracy and altruism have failed." The *Times* apparently saw nothing wrong with this. It went on to suggest that if business can do a better job in the schools than government: "Why should they not make money in the process?"

The free market approach that has produced such inequalities in the U.S. health-care system is now making inroads into one of the few areas where the U.S. provides services to all citizens: public education. According to the New York-based magazine *The Nation*, which devoted an entire issue to the situation last September, there are influential businessmen, politicians and privatization advocates who "want to supplant Thomas Jefferson's vision of a free, democratically controlled common school for all citizens with a profit-driven education marketplace."

A number of corporations have already entered the education marketplace, *The Nation* reported. Burger King has begun a chain of "Burger King Academies," fully accredited quasi-private high schools in fourteen cities. A Minneapolis company, Education Alternatives, has a contract to run public schools (for profit) in Miami, Baltimore and Duluth. And Whittle Communications, a publisher of glossy magazines for affluent consumers, has plans to launch a chain of two hundred profit-making schools by 1996.

Whittle is already familiar with the profit-making potential in the public schools. It has successfully marketed TV news-and-advertising packages to ten thousand schools across the U.S. Whittle provides the schools with free TV sets for each classroom, in exchange for a guarantee that the students will be shown a twelve-minute video that includes some "news" content as well as commercials for consumer products. With a captive market of some eight million students, Whittle is able to sell a thirty-second advertising spot for $157,000. (Following Whittle's example, a profitable Montreal-based company called Youth News Network is now trying to market a similar news-and-ad package to schools across Canada.)

But the corporate interest in the school system may go beyond profit-making; it appears to spring from a desire on the part of businessmen and other free market advocates to introduce more private-sector attitudes to the education system. This was behind the New American Schools Development Corporation (NASDC), a private initiative launched by then president George Bush and a number of prominent U.S. businessmen in 1991 to come up with innovative ideas to reform the U.S. school system. The idea was to raise $200 million from corporations to fund design teams which could, among other things, apply some corporate ideas to the education system.

These reform attempts are based on the notion that the public school system has failed miserably and must be dramatically overhauled. But education reformers outside the business community insist that the problem with American schools today is largely one of funding. "In fact, educational innovation has flourished, and educators today have a clear and proven notion of reforms that work. What's failed is basic funding for schools," write education critics Margaret Spillane and Bruce Shapiro.

This underfunding has hit the poor much harder than the rich. Schools are paid for largely by local tax dollars and each school district funds its own schools. Prosperous suburban districts pay higher local taxes and get schools that are often wonderful, with excellent facilities and a highly paid teaching staff. The inner-city schools, where there are high concentrations of poor blacks and Hispanics, have been left with a small and dwindling tax base, and therefore little to spend on education. The resulting gap between schools in some affluent areas and ones in poor, mostly black areas, is startling, as U.S. author Jonathan Kozol documents vividly in *Savage Inequalities: Children in America's Schools.*

Kozol notes that in Illinois, for instance, the poor neighbourhood of East Aurora spends $2,900 on a fourth-grade pupil in its school system, compared to $7,800 in the affluent township of Niles, near Chicago. Over the course of thirteen years of education in elementary and secondary schools, more than $100,000 will be spent educating the rich child in Niles, compared to only $38,000 educating the poor child in East Aurora.

But the numbers only tell part of the story. Kozol explores firsthand the impossible gulf between the public schools of the rich and the poor. Public School 261 in New York City, for instance, is housed in a former roller-skating rink next to a funeral home on a busy street in the North Bronx. There are 1,300 elementary school children in this bleak, windowless "school," which is supposed to have a maximum capacity of 900. Children are crowded into small windowless rooms; in one such room, four kindergarten classes share space with a sixth grade class. Lunch is eaten in three shifts of 450 students. Since there is no school yard or playground nearby, there is no recess period, and after eating lunch, children must simply sit and wait for afternoon classes to begin. There is one small gym for the whole school, twenty-six computers and about seven hundred books in the library, none of which are reference books. There is a shortage of textbooks, which children must share.

At East St. Louis High School in the grim city of East St. Louis, Illinois, the school has to be shut from time to time because of sewage backing up from the sewer system into the school's basement, and up into the kitchen areas. The school relies on some seventy "permanent substitute teachers" who are paid only $10,000 (US) a year. In the physics lab, there is no running water at the six lab stations, only empty holes where pipes were once attached. There is a football field, but it has no goalposts, except a couple of metal pipes stuck into the ground. At nearby Clark Junior High School, thirty students are crammed into a classroom only big enough for fifteen. In the boys' washroom, four of the six toilets don't work and the toilet stalls have no doors. There is no soap and no paper towels.

In affluent suburban areas, however, Kozol discovers some superbly equipped public schools. Public School 24 in the chic New York City neighbourhood of Riverdale, for instance, bears no resemblance to the public school in the North Bronx. The Riverdale school features ample lawns, with flowering bushes, a playground for small children with an elaborate jungle gym, two playing fields for older children; in addition, there are two attractive public parks in the immediate vicinity. The school's library contains 8,000 books. A large, sunny first-grade classroom contains twenty-three children, another first-grade class twenty-four. Each classroom has a computer and a sink. A sixth-grade social studies class has its own set of encyclopaedias. A fourth-grade class for ten gifted students has its own planetarium — and seven computers.

At New Trier High School in a rich suburb of Chicago, school takes on the feel of a country club. Situated on twenty-seven acres, New Trier has seven gymnasiums, an Olympic pool, a fencing room and studios for dance instruction. The school labs are fitted with the latest technology. School facilities and grounds are maintained in immaculate condition by a staff of forty-eight janitors. In addition to the full range of regular academic subjects, there is a wide variety of courses in music, art, drama, modern and classical languages, as well as aeronautics, criminal justice and computer languages. Average class size is twenty-four. Every student has a "faculty adviser" who offers personal counselling.

The spectacular quality of New Trier — and the horrors of East St. Louis High — are directly related to the wealth of the local communities around the schools. New Trier has a property tax base that is five times as high as that of other schools in the Chicago area, and residents in the New Trier district have consistently voted against proposals to redistribute school funds to help the poorer areas. They have created, in effect, a private school within the public school system.

The gap between the health and education services available to the rich and those available to the poor in the U.S. is a discrepancy that is largely absent in Europe, where high-level services are available to all.

This only accentuates another great discrepancy in the U.S. — the gap between the incomes of the rich and the poor. This income inequality, which is also far more pronounced in the U.S. than in Europe, grew considerably in the U.S. throughout the '80s under the neoconservative economic policies of the Reagan and Bush administrations. The biggest gains by far went to the top 1 per cent of Americans, according to data released in March 1992 by the Congressional Budget Office, the research arm of Congress. The data showed that between 1977 and 1989, income expanded for all Americans by a total of $740 billion, and an astonishing $550 billion of this — 74 per cent — went to the top 1 per cent of U.S. families. The incomes of this tiny élite of 600,000 families grew from an average of $315,000 to $560,000 over the twelve-year period (in inflation-adjusted US dollars).

Meanwhile, the typical American family — earning the median income — experienced an increase of only 4 per cent to $36,000. People at the low end of the scale actually saw their incomes decline, the Congressional data found.

As the income discrepancies increased in American society, most Americans also saw their social benefits decline. This is because the U.S. emphasis on the private market approach to social welfare leaves most middle-class people dependent on their employers for benefits. Since government provides few social benefits and the cost of buying them privately is often exorbitant, workers generally try to negotiate social benefits in the workplace, either through union contracts or through private arrangements. This means that workers' social benefits — everything from health care to pension benefits to maternity leave — are often directly connected to their jobs. Among other things, this has the effect of concentrating enormous power in the hands of employers.

So when employers try to cut costs — such as during a recession — employee benefits are an obvious target. "As companies seek to control rising costs of medical and pension plans, they are increasingly making changes in benefits packages that reduce the dollar value of the coverage, and at the same time shift the cost to employees," noted *The Wall Street Journal* in November 1992.

Some of the most bitter strikes in the U.S. in recent years have been over company attempts to reduce benefits. Employers are also increasingly trying to entice employees to voluntarily give up benefits in exchange for cash. Nearly three-quarters of U.S. companies offer employees the option of giving up medical coverage for themselves and their families, generally in exchange for cash payments ranging from $300 to $900, according to *The Wall Street Journal*. This cash bonus may be particularly appealing to families where both spouses have jobs with medical plans. But relying on the spouse's medical plan can be dangerous — if the spouse becomes unemployed or the marriage breaks up. An employee who tries to rejoin the company's medical plan may find it impossible to do so, particularly if the employee's health has deteriorated in the meantime and the insurance company refuses to offer coverage, as is often the case.

The shift to part-time work has also contributed to the decline of employee benefits. During the '80s, there was a decline in the number of full-time, unionized jobs and an increase in the number of part-time, non-unionized jobs. These part-time jobs not only generally pay less, but they offer fewer benefits. Indeed, this shift to jobs with poor — or non-existent — benefits helps explain why the number of Americans without any health insurance grew from 14.6 per cent of the U.S. population in 1979 to 17.5 per cent in 1985, according to Navarro, the health economist from Johns Hopkins.

Dependence on job-related benefits has also left American workers doubly vulnerable to unemployment, since the loss of a job not only eliminates income but also leaves worker and family without crucial benefits. "To be unemployed is a much worse situation in the United States than in any other

Western capitalist society," says Navarro. He argues that this has been a crucial factor in encouraging workers to accept concessions, rather than face the terror of unemployment.

The free market approach also pervades the way the U.S. deals with the poor. Since the mainstream American view holds that the free market functions fairly and requires little intervention by government, the poor present a particular problem. Why aren't they able to take care of themselves?

In popular mythology, the U.S. is the land of opportunity, the land where penniless immigrants can work hard and save and even, with enough diligence, become millionaires. There are no external barriers standing in their way, like the stultifying class systems that so many Europeans came to America to escape over the last century.

Despite the continuing popularity of this image of America, there is in fact less upward mobility in the U.S. today than in many European countries. A recent study by the Joint Center for Political and Economic Studies in Washington examined poverty in the U.S. and seven other industrialized countries and found that poverty in America is more pervasive, more severe and more long-term. Indeed, the study found that there was considerably less upward mobility in the U.S. than in any of the other countries. "Virtually all poor families in West Germany, Luxembourg and the Netherlands were able to raise their incomes above the poverty level," according to the study. "In the United States, however, 1 in 7 families was consistently poor over at least the three years observed in the study."

The presence of a large and seemingly permanent underclass is a rude affront to the American dream. And Americans have largely dealt with that reality by finding deficiencies in the poor. Rather than consider that there might be something wrong with their system, they have decided that there's something wrong with their poor. The problem is only compounded by the fact that so many of the poor are black and Hispanic, allowing racial stereotypes to reinforce white middle-class conclusions that the poor are somehow inadequate.

"The attitude is that people are poor because they behave badly," says Katherine McFate, senior research associate with the Joint Center. McFate describes Americans as "punitive" towards the poor. Recent cuts to state welfare programs included new rules designed to punish single mothers on welfare who have additional children. The state of Wisconsin, for instance, decided to reduce benefit levels for a second child and cut off additional benefits for a third child entirely.

The hostility to the poor in the U.S. can perhaps best be seen through the eyes of Jessie Morgan, a nineteen-year-old cerebral palsy victim in Santa Rosa, California. Morgan, who has been confined to a wheelchair all her life, ended up sleeping on the floor of the local national guard armoury after she was evicted from her apartment and failed to qualify for a subsidized housing complex. Her shocking story only came to public attention in January 1992 because of an unusual twist — the local humane society took away her dog because it considered a national guard armoury an inappropriate home for a dog!

When I reached her by telephone, Jessie Morgan was almost indifferent to her own plight; her main concern was that her dog had been taken away. She seemed oblivious to the larger question of why a severely disabled person living in one of the richest countries in the world would find herself faced with a choice between sleeping on the floor of a military barracks and sleeping on the street.

Indeed, she was quite defensive. She said she knew the national guard armoury wasn't the best place for a dog and she was trying to find better accommodation. But she repeatedly said that she was a responsible guardian for the dog and *not some lazy welfare recipient*. "I am not sitting on my butt doing nothing," she insisted. The notion that the poor are responsible for their plight is so prevalent in the U.S. that even a cerebral palsy victim, confined throughout her life to a wheelchair, felt obliged to explain that her homelessness was not her fault.

Another American response to poverty is to deny its existence. This is the attitude, for instance, at the Heritage Foundation, which puts out booklets suggesting that the plight of the poor in the U.S. is not so bad. From his office at the Heritage Foundation in the U.S. capital — a city virtually encircled with wretched ghettos — foundation analyst Robert Rector elaborates on this theme. "There's little poverty in the U.S. in the sense of inadequate housing or people being badly fed."

Rector trots out a number of comparisons to suggest that the American poor aren't that badly off compared to the poor in other countries. He notes, for instance, that America's poor have less protein deficiency than poor people in India and Bangladesh. What's astonishing about this line of argument is the indifference to the fact that the U.S. is one of the richest countries in the world and therefore presumably better able than Bangladesh to care for its poor.

Indeed, the discrepancy in resources between the U.S. and Bangladesh makes the findings of a report in the *New England Journal of Medicine* particularly striking. The January 1990 report found that, while Americans in general are far more likely to reach the age of sixty-five than are residents of Bangladesh, this is not the case with poor Americans living in New York City's Harlem district. Indeed, as noted earlier, black men in Harlem are less likely to reach the age of sixty-five than men in Bangladesh.

While some of the difference was attributed to higher rates of violence and drug abuse in Harlem, the study found that most of it was due to other health-related factors, such as cardiovascular disease. The authors of the study, Dr. Colin McCord and

Dr. Harold P. Freeman, concluded that Harlem and probably other U.S. inner-city areas justify special consideration similar to that given to areas hit by natural disasters. "A major political and financial commitment will be needed," they argued, "to eradicate the root causes of this high mortality: vicious poverty and inadequate access to the basic health care that is the right of all Americans."

At the Washington office of the Child Welfare League of America, executive director David S. Liederman chokes on his juice when he hears of arguments churned out by the Heritage Foundation. "You'd have to be living on another planet not to know what the problems of poverty are in this country...We really do have a national crisis on our hands," says Liederman. "It's fine for some well-salaried person at the Heritage Foundation to sit around playing with numbers and dream up ways to do behaviour modification." Liederman argues that part of the problem is the failure of Americans to look for solutions beyond their own borders. "People here think the sun rises and sets on the U.S. We have a lot to learn from our friends."

Certainly the Europeans do things differently. But just how differently — and how much better — they do things in Europe is a subject that we in North America still know surprisingly little about.

# 4

## Europe's Little Secret

$A$blank look came over the face of the woman I was interviewing. A professor in Sweden's Centre for Working Life, Annika Baude had been active for years in the social policy area, having played a key role in the development and expansion of Sweden's day-care system in the '70s. But while she spoke very good English, she suddenly looked quizzical, as if she hadn't understood something I'd just said.

"Food banks?" she asked. "What's that?"

The gulf between Sweden and Canada came sharply into relief for me, perhaps for the first time since my arrival several days earlier in Stockholm. I had been struck, of course, by the cleanliness and well-maintained look of the city, as well as by the apparently healthy and well-educated populace. But it wasn't until then that I realized just how different things really were. As a Canadian, I had become so familiar with food banks that I had lost sight of the fact that not all countries in the world consider it civilized for large segments of the population to rely on private charity to feed themselves and their families.

When I explained what food banks were, she seemed genuinely surprised — especially when I told her that hundreds of thousands of Canadians depend on them for regular nourishment.

Annika Baude was even more surprised to hear that there were homeless people in Canada.

"In such a cold country?" she asked. "Where do they sleep?"

When I found myself describing people sleeping over grates or huddled in alcoves, I was struck anew by the horror of what I was saying. I'd seen people like this myself on winter nights in downtown Toronto — nights that were so cold that I could hardly bear to walk a short distance in a warm coat. I was hard-pressed to explain how these people managed to survive in such a cold country. I pointed out that every now and then a homeless person dies, and it makes a small item in the press. I remembered driving on the highway that runs from Baltimore to Washington, and seeing a poster — obviously not put there by the government — which read: "Welcome to the nation's capital, where the homeless die."

I certainly hadn't seen anyone homeless on the streets of Stockholm. Even the poorest part of town — Rinkaby — was clean and well maintained with open fruit and vegetable markets, fast-food outlets and modest but decent low-rise apartment complexes. The subway stop for Rinkaby was as clean and well kept as the others throughout the Stockholm subway system. Like other subway stops, it had elevators so that elderly people and women with baby carriages don't have to use the escalators.

Sweden, of course, is the social welfare model of Europe. But the simple truth is that western Europe does things differently than we do in North America. It would be wrong to romanticize Europe, which has been the site of horrific wars, and continues to be full of injustices, inequalities, as well as current violent hostilities. But it is equally wrong to ignore — as we have in recent decades — what Europeans do better than us. One thing that they appear to do considerably better is to make efforts to provide a decent standard of living for all.

One of the best-kept secrets in North America is the benefits that are available in European countries. Despite the vast information we receive in the media here about European politics and trade negotiations, one thing we almost never hear about is what superior benefits Europeans enjoy — how extensive their day-care systems are, how much longer their holidays are, what generous family benefits they enjoy, what excellent public transit systems they have, what better labour training programs they offer.

It would be beyond the scope of this little book to attempt to deal with all these areas. Instead, we'll just explore briefly how much support the European countries offer in an activity that almost everyone engages in: raising a family. For added interest, we'll then compare the European benefits to those available in the U.S. and Canada.

To set the stage, here's an overview observation by Sheila Kamerman, a professor of social planning who specializes in international comparisons of family policy at Columbia University's School of Social Work: "To an American observer, the European commitment to working parents and their children is nothing short of astonishing."

Indeed, in virtually every area, European countries provide far greater benefits for families. If we take four key areas that affect the family — parental leave, child benefits, child care, and health care — we can see a strong pattern in the advanced countries of western Europe and Scandinavia that diverges sharply from the pattern in the United States.

The western European countries provide paid maternity leave for all working women, as do in fact one hundred countries around the world.

The systems vary from country to country, but the essence of the European maternity leave policies are the same: the woman's job and benefits are guaranteed and she receives a significant portion of her former income while on leave. The leave periods range from three months in Portugal to a full year in Sweden, with five or six months being the average. The benefit levels vary too, with Greece, for instance, covering only 50 per cent of a woman's previous salary, and richer countries like Germany, France, Sweden and Denmark paying 90 to 100 per cent. (In many countries, these benefits are actually tax-free.)

In addition, some countries, such as Austria, Germany, Norway, Denmark and Sweden, also provide some form of parental leave for fathers. These generous leave policies thus offer parents the opportunity for time with newly arrived children — without significant loss of family income.

The Scandinavian countries are particularly advanced in the area of parental leave, with Sweden offering a highly flexible package of leaves for both parents for up to fifteen months. "A working mother might take off a full six months; she and her husband might then each work half-time for nine months, sharing child care between them; or they might each work three-quarters time for one year, without significant pay loss," says Kamerman.

The U.S., on the other hand, provides only unpaid maternity leave. This puts the U.S. once again into the company of South Africa, as the only two industrialized nations that offer no maternity benefits. "The principal difference between the American working mother and her counterpart in the rest of the industrialized world is that the American woman gets virtually no help. She's on her own," says Kamerman.

Indeed, in the past, American women weren't even entitled to unpaid leave. However, a new law signed by President Clinton after years of resistance by the Bush administration provides 12 weeks of unpaid maternity leave. But millions of American women still won't qualify for even this unpaid leave, since the new law does not apply to workers in small businesses (with less than 50 employees).

Canada falls somewhere between the advanced countries of Europe and the U.S., offering a fifteen-week benefit period at 57 per cent of previous earnings plus an option of an additional ten weeks of parental leave for fathers or mothers. This is considerably less generous than the major European countries, but slightly more generous than Greece, for instance. And it obviously is more generous than the U.S., which offers no financial support.

All the European countries provide some form of family benefits package to assist families with the cost of raising children.

The packages vary from country to country, but certain patterns emerge. Once again, we find Sweden, France and Germany scoring high in terms of generosity of benefits. Kamerman, along with another social policy professor at Columbia University, Alfred Kahn, carried out an exhaustive study comparing overall benefits* received by many different types of families in these European countries, as well as several other countries, including the United States and Canada. Their findings reveal a significant gap between the support enjoyed by European families and that available to American — and Canadian — families.

---

* Including direct payments as well as tax benefits.

Sweden, which emerges as probably the most generous in the area of family support, provides a mix of benefits that gives the unemployed single mother, for instance, a level of income roughly double that found in countries like Canada and the U.S. Interestingly, the Swedish package relies far less on welfare payments and more on child support and housing allowances. "Swedish single mothers are not poor," notes Kamerman. "Female labour force participation rates are high and social benefits are extensive, generous and available." This generosity is applied virtually across the board, to many different family types. Sweden, for instance, pays parents a child allowance equivalent to roughly $150 per child per month, with supplements for families with three or more children, until the child reaches sixteen, or older if still in school.

France, which is in some areas even more generous than Sweden, also relies relatively little on welfare benefits. Instead, it has a rich system of family allowance payments and housing allowances. All families receive a monthly family allowance of roughly $200, beginning six months *before* the birth of the child, and continuing for three months after birth. Most families continue to receive this benefit until the child is three years old. (Although this part is an income-tested benefit, roughly 80 per cent of families qualify to receive it.) In addition, larger families receive benefits of $150 a month per child (more for a third or subsequent child) until the age of sixteen (or older, if still in school). Like Sweden, France also offers a housing allowance, based on need; roughly one-quarter of French families receive it. Additional benefits are available for single mothers.

Germany, which also scores relatively high in generosity, provides a basic monthly family allowance of $57 for the first child, $106 for the second, $180 for the third, $196 for the fourth child and subsequent children. Thus, a family with three children would receive a monthly family allowance totalling $343. (High-income families receive somewhat lower payments; a high-income family with three children would, for instance, receive a monthly allowance of $228.) Germany also offers housing allowances. Its benefits to single mothers are less generous than those in Sweden and France, but it does offer them a government child support payment, if the absent father fails to make his support payments. (These government child support benefits are also available in Sweden and France.)

In the United States, on the other hand, there are no universal child benefits, nor housing allowances for families with children, and child-support arrangements are often poorly enforced. Instead, there is a patchwork of programs, mostly run by individual states, all directed exclusively at the poor. "If you're poor, some things are available to you, although not enough," explains Pat Maunsell of the Family Resource Coalition in Chicago. "If you're middle-class, there's far less. You're basically out there on your own." But not even all poor families qualify for assistance in the U.S. Some states, for instance, refuse to provide any benefits for families with two parents, leaving them with no support except federal food stamp vouchers.

The main source of support for poor U.S. families is a welfare program called Aid to Families with Dependent Children (AFDC), which is directed almost exclusively at single mothers. Since benefit levels and eligibility requirements are set by each individual state, there is tremendous variation. In her international study, Kamerman looked at support levels in two states, New York and Pennsylvania, both relatively generous compared to other U.S. states. (A family of three received $577 [US] in monthly AFDC benefits in New York and $421 [US] in Pennsylvania in 1992, whereas the typical or median state offered a benefit of only $367 [US] a month for such a family.) Had Kamerman selected a more typical state, the U.S. would have looked worse in her international comparisons. However, even using these two "generous" states, the U.S. ranked considerably below the European countries in its generosity to families.

Once again, Canada is nudged between Europe and the U.S., but closer to the U.S. Kamerman's international comparisons show that Canada is more generous than the U.S., but considerably less generous than Europe. Lacking the housing and family allowances of Europe, we rely heavily on welfare payments. And, as Kamerman shows, we do particularly poorly in helping the most vulnerable families. In fact, in this category we score slightly worse than even the state of New York.

In the area of day care, most European countries are quite a bit ahead of North America, although there are still some important gaps.

For children under three, the European record is somewhat spotty, with most parents making private arrangements. The exception to this is Sweden, which offers high-quality public child care from the age of about one year, allowing parents to put their child in day care as soon as paid maternity leave runs out. Parents pay a small fee, but most of the costs are subsidized by the state.

But once a child is three (or two and a half in some countries), most European countries offer "preschool," which amounts to a public nursery school system. In France, which has a particularly impressive public system, more than 95 per cent of children three and older attend the full-day program, including many whose mothers do not work.

The preschools are free and the quality of programs is high. Teachers must have an equivalent of a master's degree in early childhood education. Preschools are located in attractive buildings that are designed and used exclusively for children. Day-long programs include language arts, crafts, games, dance, singing, rest and play. The children regularly go on outings, including "green classes" where they travel to the countryside to visit farms and cheese factories. In keeping with the spirit of France, they even offer "gourmet" meals, complete with appetizers.

"The schools have one objective — to get kids to fall in love with school," says Nell Rivière-Platt, an American who teaches French social policy to foreign government trainees at a private college in Paris. Rivière-Platt, whose two children both attended the nursery schools, known as Écoles Maternelles, says that her son's class even went for free pony riding lessons.

The French child-care system dazzled a team of U.S. child-care professionals who spent two weeks in France in 1989 on a fact-finding trip sponsored by the French-American Foundation. "We found a country at a level of economic development similar to that of the United States but far ahead of us in ensuring that its young children are well and safely cared for," according to a report by the fourteen-member team, which included in its ranks doctors, academics and child-care administrators. Notably, it also included lawyer and child-welfare activist Hillary Rodham Clinton, who at the time was just one of many experts on the team, but now, as wife of U.S. President Bill Clinton, turns out to be its most influential member.

The team's report, which lavished praise on the French system while drawing attention to inadequacies in the U.S. system, concluded that the greater amount the French spend on early childhood education is money well spent. "Society eventually pays for its inadequate care of children in their later school failures, substance abuse, delinquency, wasted work lives, and uninformed citizenship," the report argues.

In contrast to the child-care system in France and in other European countries, the U.S. child-care system is virtually non-existent. One of the few federal initiatives is a program called Head Start, which is aimed at helping the most disadvantaged children get preparation for school. But once again, not all the poor have access to this program targeted specifically at the poor. For instance, despite the severe poverty in the North Bronx in New York City, few children there are enrolled in the Head Start program, largely because the severely overcrowded schools have no room to accommodate them.

Most Americans choose between a hodge-podge of small, non-profit day-care centres, run by social service organizations and church groups, or an assortment of private, profit-making day-care centres, including large day-care chains. Indeed, day care in the U.S. is big business. Children's World Learning Centers, the third-largest child-care company in the U.S., for instance, is a division of ARA Group, a huge closely held company which operates everything from park concessions to uniform rental services and boasts more than $4 billion a year in revenues.

It is hard to piece together an overview of the U.S. day-care situation, since it varies so much from state to state, says Mary Lee Allen, a spokesperson for the Children's Defense Fund in Washington. A six-month investigation of child-care centres in Minnesota by the St. Paul *Pioneer Press* found consistent evidence of poor-quality care, particularly among the large chains, where corners were often cut to keep expenses down. The newspaper reported 1,700 charges of violations of state licensing regulations in the chains' 114 centres during a six-month period, including violations of child-staff ratio regulations, inadequate building maintenance and poor nutrition. Snacks often consisted of nothing but water and a cracker, the paper reported.

For many working parents in the U.S., day-care centres are an unaffordable luxury. Parents are often obliged to leave even very young children in cheaper, unregulated arrangements with neighbours or others. Says Kamerman: "The U.S. has more very young infants (under three months) in poor quality out-of-home child-care arrangements than does any other major industrialized country."

All the countries of western Europe have essentially achieved universal health coverage. Systems vary from country to country. In Sweden, for instance, patients must generally pay a small user fee for each visit to the doctor. On the other hand, Swedish public health insurance covers many things not covered by Canada's medicare system. For instance, the Swedish system pays part of the cost of prescription drugs, including birth control pills, and pays the full cost of drugs for serious or chronic illnesses. It also pays 40 per cent of dental bills, and 100 per cent of dental bills for children up to the age of nineteen.

The United States, as we've seen, does not have universal health coverage and, as a result, access to proper health care can be difficult to attain for those without sufficient resources. This leaves the U.S. virtually alone in the industrialized world — along with South Africa — in its failure to provide health care at least to all pregnant women and their children.

Indeed, it is not unusual for women in the U.S. to receive no prenatal care — a fact which helps explain the surprisingly high U.S. rate of infant mortality (deaths of infants under the age of one). The United States has a poorer record than almost all European countries in infant mortality, which the World Health Organization has described as a useful measure of not only infant health, but the health of the whole population. Among European nations, only Portugal and Greece have worse infant mortality records.

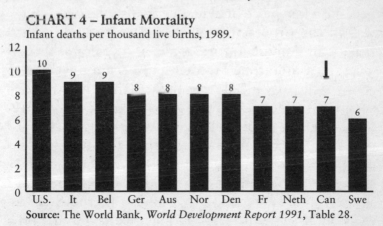

**CHART 4 – Infant Mortality**
Infant deaths per thousand live births, 1989.

**Source:** The World Bank, *World Development Report 1991*, Table 28.

83

"Many Americans comfort themselves with the belief that, even if their system is by far the most costly and least equitable of any in the industrialized democracies, at least it provides 'the world's best care' for those who can afford it," notes Robert G. Evans, a health economist at the University of British Columbia. Evans says that the evidence does not bear this out. "What America provides is not the world's best, but the world's most, and most highly priced."

\* \* \* \* \* \*

When Sweden's minister of schools announced a program in 1991 to fund private schools, many foreign commentators took the move as evidence that the bastion of social democray was about to crumble.

Private schools seemed to represent the antithesis of everything that social democratic, egalitarian Sweden stood for, and Sweden's move to fund them became a key piece of evidence that social democracy was in the process of self-destructing. Some North American commentators could hardly conceal their glee: for a long time Sweden had been a nuisance to those who advanced the theory that large social spending stifled economic growth and competitiveness. There was Sweden, with its very high standard of living, a corporate sector that was world-class competitive (to borrow a phrase), and a huge welfare state strongly committed to equality. But the defeat of the Social Democratic government in the Swedish election of September 1991 at last seemed to herald a change of direction. Commentators who had rarely mentioned Sweden in the past suddenly rushed to Stockholm and wrote articles about the end of social democracy.

But the changes were often more subtle than the commentators portrayed. For instance, in announcing the decision to fund private schools, Beatrice Ask, the new minister of schools, made two important stipulations: that the curriculum would be set by government and that private schools receiving government funds *would no longer be allowed to charge tuition fees* — thereby removing the financial barrier that generally serves to keep private schools the preserve of the rich. She declared that good schooling should not be a function of the parent's ability to pay, and that Sweden would not tolerate a two-tiered system, with better schools available to those who could pay more. Thus the move, while significant, was not really the assault on the welfare state that it may have seemed at first. Like many things that are happening in Sweden — the most advanced social welfare state in the world — the move had more to do with improving the flexibility of the welfare state than attacking its scope, size or purpose.

Even conservative commentators within Sweden acknowledge that the defeat of the Social Democrats in the September 1991 election should not be interpreted as a popular desire to dismantle the welfare state. "Swedish people want their welfare state," said Mattias Bengtsson, an editorial writer and columnist for *Svenska Dagbladet*, Stockholm's conservative daily. "If you ask people if they are in favour of the welfare state or not, the answer is yes."

Bengtsson explains that the long-ruling Social Democrats lost power to a coalition dominated by the Conservative Party, or Moderate Party as it is often called, because Swedes felt that the welfare state was not delivering enough of what they wanted. A big part of the reform thrust of the new government has been to make the Swedish welfare state more responsive — allowing people, for instance, to choose their own doctors and to set up private day-care centres and schools. The emphasis has been on providing more choice within systems that are still universally accessible, publicly funded and fully regulated.

This is a far cry from the minimal welfare state that has developed in the United States, where the government does little to provide, fund or regulate social welfare. Certainly the refusal of the new Conservative government in Sweden to allow the development of two-tiered social systems shows it adheres to a social philosophy far different from that of conservatives in the U.S., where a multi-tiered system is tolerated — even apparently considered appropriate — in areas as important as health care and education.

Indeed, while there is a minority in Sweden's Conservative party who want to dramatically cut back the welfare state, this is not the mainstream view of the party, which is made up of "social" conservatives who are by and large sympathetic to the welfare state. "The [new government] did not gain power by promising to dismantle the universal programs," notes Bo Rothstein, a professor in the government studies department of Uppsala University in Sweden. "In fact, the party now responsible for the Ministry of Health and Social Affairs, the Liberal Party, has time and again declared its loyalty to the principles of the universal welfare state." Indeed, in the past, the Liberal party often sided with the Social Democrats on social legislation.

"There'll be no big cuts as long as the Liberal party is part of the coalition," Carl-Anders Ifvarsson, a Liberal who is under-secretary of state in the Ministry of Health and Social Affairs, said in an interview in Stockholm. Ifvarsson says that there is a "broad consensus that we don't want a bigger gap between rich and poor in Sweden."

In recent months, Swedish government finances have been under increased pressure due to an economic slowdown, a currency crisis in the fall of 1992, and a costly government bail-out of the banking industry, which had financed a real estate speculation boom in the '80s. To stem the currency crisis and prevent a devaluation of the kronor, the ruling Conservative coalition concluded an unusual deal with the opposition Social Democrats in October that will reduce social expenditure somewhat as well as cut back spending in defence and foreign aid.

Just how serious the cuts will be in the social welfare domain remains to be seen. In the area of child benefits, for instance, the deal between the coalition and the Social Democrats cancelled a planned increase in benefits that was scheduled to take place in January 1993. Kamerman, who follows Sweden closely, says that so far "the changes have been largely at the margin." She says that while they may be significant for Swedes, they do not affect the overall place of Sweden as an international leader in the field of social welfare.

Furthermore, the October deal gives the Social Democrats veto power over important aspects of the government's labour market policy, which has long been considered a key element in the Swedish welfare state. Traditionally, the Swedish government has taken an activist role in labour market policies, striving for full employment through extensive government job training and job placement services, and the creation of public works projects to provide jobs for the unemployed. Indeed, many Swedish commentators argue that Sweden's low unemployment rate has been crucial to its success as a generous welfare state, since it has meant the vast majority of Swedes are working and paying taxes rather than draining government revenues by living on welfare or unemployment benefits. With the Social Democrats retaining veto power over labour market policy in their deal with the Conservatives, they have managed to hold onto a key lever in the Swedish welfare state.

The financial pressures felt in Sweden have been felt to various degrees throughout Europe. The slower economic growth experienced in the industrial world since the oil crisis of the early 1970s has placed limits on the growth of social programs in many European countries. Furthermore, there have been attempts to eliminate inefficiencies in certain programs, particularly those dealing with disability and sickness, where too many healthy individuals were found to be claiming benefits.

But none of this appears to amount to a weakening of commitment to the welfare state. Indeed, there seems to be less questioning in Sweden and the other advanced welfare states in Scandinavia and continental Europe of the importance of maintaining extensive social welfare systems. "During the economic crisis in the '70s, there were questions raised about social security and its financing," says Taoufik Bendahou, a social security specialist in the UN-affiliated International Labour Office (ILO) in Geneva. "But we seem to have passed this point. I don't see any erosion of social protections. . . . I don't think there is anybody now who can question the importance of social protection."

For many in Europe that commitment was only strengthened by the spectacle of the riots in Los Angeles in the spring of 1992. Guy Standing, an ILO analyst, argues that the L.A. riots showed that the cost of doing without a welfare state is a disconnected underclass, cut off from mainstream society.

"Watching those scenes of people living on the edge of civilization was astonishing," he said. "That's what happens when you deprive people of appropriate education, sanitation, health care . . . when people don't have any hope."

So despite recessionary times, there are few calls for serious cutbacks in the welfare state. "In Scandinavia, you'd no more say 'cut back the welfare state' than you'd say 'stop producing publicly owned roads,' " says Edwin Bell, a policy analyst at the Paris headquarters of the Organization of Economic Co-operation and Development.

While European social programs have survived the ravages of the recession of the '80s, they face another hurdle as Europe moves to become a single market in 1993. Some fear that this will place a downward pressure on social programs, as the rich nations of Europe find themselves in a common trading bloc with the low-wage southern European countries of Greece, Portugal and Spain — much as Canada would face pressure in a trading bloc with Mexico.

While it is too soon to tell what the outcome will be, there are important differences between the North American and European situations. Unlike the North American countries, the nations of the European Community (EC) are taking steps to raise the standards in the low-wage countries by requiring rich EC nations to make substantial equalization payments to the poorer ones, and also by establishing a social charter that aims to enforce uniform labour standards in all EC countries.

The social charter, which was adopted by all twelve EC countries except Britain, defines basic rights for all workers, including rights to decent wages, union membership and collective bargaining, vocational training, equal treatment of men and women and guarantees of workplace health and safety. So, while corporations will be free to locate in low-wage countries, they won't be able to exploit the kind of sweatshop conditions that exist, for instance, in Mexico. Thus there will be less incentive for capital to move to the low-wage countries – a move that would jeopardize the tax base and wage levels of the richer nations.

Furthermore, Europeans start off their single-market experiment with a much stronger commitment to social programs than do the countries of North America. Jacques Delors, president of the EC Commission and a key promoter of the social charter, argues that the real purpose of moving to a single European market is to rebuild the conditions for a "European model of society," combining a dynamic economy with an extensive welfare state.

To a far greater extent than in North America, social welfare in Europe has been a consensus issue, with conservatives and social democrats both playing a role in providing social welfare benefits to the public. Much of France's generous child-benefits system, for instance, was put in place by conservative French governments. Similarly, the extensive German pension system was pioneered in the last century by conservative leaders like Otto von Bismarck.

In almost all the advanced welfare states of Europe, it was conservative forces with roots in the Catholic Church and hierarchical feudal systems of the past who first championed state programs providing benefits for workers, notes Gosta Esping-Andersen. These conservative forces felt threatened by the new forces of both socialism and capitalism that had been unleashed by the Industrial Revolution. They saw programs that ensured decent standards for the emerging working class as a way of preserving social stability — and their privileged position in the status quo.

This paternalistic approach contrasts sharply with that of U.S. élites, whose dominance was based not on hierarchical traditions but on the power they wielded in the private marketplace. Thus, U.S. business has had little interest in constraining the free play of the market. Indeed, U.S. business has "tended to view every piece of social or labour legislation as something that must be stopped to prevent us from going down the road to socialism," says Larry Mishel of the Economic Policy Institute in Washington.

But the future of social programs in Europe may depend more than anything on the strength of the European labour movement and its ability to adapt to the new political situation. Certainly, it was the powerful labour movements that emerged in Europe in the late ninteenth century that became the key force behind the push for universal social programs. (Similarly, the lack of a strong labour movement in the U.S. explains why the United States failed to develop a national health insurance plan, as well as other social welfare programs, according to Vicente Navarro from Johns Hopkins University.)

The strong union movements in Europe pushed for universal social programs to improve the conditions of their members, and also to prevent splits in the working class. They feared that the power of unionized labour would be undermined by the presence of a huge pool of unemployed workers who, desperate and without benefits, would sabotage strikes and work for lower wages. The strong influence of labour is evident in the European practice of long vacation periods. In Sweden, the legal annual leave is five weeks, and many Swedes, including civil servants, get seven weeks. In most European countries the annual leave ranges from four to six weeks, compared to just two weeks in Canada and the United States.

The universal approach to social welfare was, as we've seen, developed to its most sophisticated level in Scandinavia, where labour was particularly strong. Esping-Andersen puts the Scandinavians into a class of their own when he classifies the welfare states of the industrialized world. He identifies three models — the Anglo-American model, best typified by the minimal welfare states of the United States and Britain under Margaret Thatcher (he also lumps Canada and Australia into this category), the continental European model, with more extensive social welfare systems that are partly the work of paternalistic conservative governments, and finally the advanced social welfare states of Scandinavia.

The Scandinavians have gone the farthest towards developing the notion of "social citizenship," where a high level of social welfare is a right enjoyed by everyone. In this sense, Sweden is the most genuinely middle-class society.

The reach of the Swedish welfare state seems truly extraordinary to the North American observer. Annika Baude describes the extent of the care provided by municipal social services to her ninety-four-year-old aunt, who lived until her recent death in a suburb of Stockholm. "Every day there would be home help. Someone brought her coffee, someone brought her lunch. They washed her and made her bed each day and later someone would bring her the evening paper and make her dinner. When she developed an open sore on her back, a nurse came every day," says Baude.

Such extensive services require a large bureaucracy. But this fits well with Sweden's commitment to full employment. With its active labour market policies, unemployment rates hovered around 3 per cent throughout the '80s, while European and North American rates were considerably higher, even in some cases rising above 10 per cent. The current Swedish unemployment rate of 6.5 per cent seems unduly high to many Swedes.

Sweden's commitment to full employment reflects a strong belief in the work ethic. Contrary to the popular North American image of welfare states as breeding grounds for laziness, here in the world capital of social welfare, there is little tolerance for idleness. The Swedes expect people to work and the Swedish government goes to considerable lengths to make sure that there are jobs available, and that Swedes are trained to do them. Unemployment insurance funds are mostly run by trade unions, which take a dim view of able-bodied workers being idle. The labour force participation rates of women — including single mothers — is among the highest in the world.

It should be noted that this is all carried out in an economy where the major enterprises are largely privately owned. The Swedish welfare state has developed and flourished within a strongly capitalist environment. Attempts to go beyond this in the '70s — to move towards greater worker control of the economy — were strongly rebuffed by the powerful Swedish business class.

The importance of full employment remains central to the Swedish welfare concept. Certainly, Swedes cringe at the prospect of unemployment levels that we have become used to in Canada — above 11 per cent, not including workers who have given up after long periods of fruitless job search. Says Rudolf Meidner, a distinguished Swedish economist and architect of the welfare state: "You [in Canada] are living in a situation we would find catastrophic."

Of course, many Canadians do find the Canadian situation catastrophic. And they were probably surprised last fall when, night after night, they saw television commericals boasting that the United Nations had ranked Canada number one in its international measure of "human development." The Mulroney government had launched a massive and costly advertising campaign to publicize the UN's decision, in an apparent attempt to convince disgruntled Canadians that maybe Ottawa wasn't doing such a bad job after all. But, as we will see in the next chapter, the government wasn't telling us the whole story.

# 5

# CANADA TRIUMPHANT: JUST DON'T READ THE FINE PRINT

With the Toronto Blue Jays out in front in the World Series in October 1992, it seemed somehow only appropriate that Canada should also lead the world in human development.

Certainly it was difficult to watch a World Series game on TV last fall without repeatedly seeing the commercial reminding Canadians that the UN had placed Canada at the top of its international list measuring "human development." In the three years since the United Nations has been coming out with its rankings, Canada has always hovered around the top. But last year was the first year that we actually inched into first place.

The ranking was also the first bit of good news for the Mulroney government in a long time — especially attractive because many Canadians had come to see the Tories as the party responsible for dismantling Canada's social welfare system. Yet here was the top body in the world suggesting that Canada was a great place to live. Ottawa wasted no time in trumpeting the news, buying up so much airtime during the World Series that most fans came to dislike the commercials as much as the tomahawk chop.

But, on closer examination, the results of the UN report card are less impressive — as the UN report itself points out.

The report measures indicators of human development in the areas of health, education and national income. All the Western industrialized nations excel in the education category, as measured by adult literacy and years of schooling, with the U.S. slightly ahead of the pack. But the U.S. loses ground in the health category, as measured by life expectancy at birth, largely because of the inadequate U.S. health-care system. Canada and the European countries, with their stronger health-care systems, pull into the lead. In the final analysis, Canada inches into first place on the basis of higher national income, as measured in purchasing power. Canada, like the U.S., has higher purchasing power than the European countries.

But it is important to recognize what this means. This does not mean, as some might think, that the average Canadian and American citizen necessarily has greater purchasing power than does the average European citizen. What it does mean is that if you add up the purchasing power of all individuals in each country and then divide that amount by the number of people in the country, Canada and the United States score a higher number than the European countries. What is camouflaged in such a calculation is any indication of how a country's national income total is divided *among* its citizens.

The United Arab Emirates, for instance, ranks at the top of the UN's measure of per capita purchasing power. This isn't a reflection of a high standard of living or strong purchasing power for the ordinary citizen there. Indeed, the United Arab Emirates ranks poorly in life expectancy, and almost half its population is illiterate, according to the UN report. Its high score in national income is nothing more than an indication that some enormously wealthy individuals, presumably oil sheiks, are pulling up the national average. Similarly, Canadian and American per capita incomes are high partly because there is tremendous income among the rich.

But having a richer group at the top doesn't necessarily tell us much about the level of human development in a country. The UN recognizes this problem and has set out to correct it by including an additional chart, measuring income inequality, or what is often referred to as a country's "income distribution." This gives a clearer picture of how the ordinary citizen fares. In this measure of income inequality, Canada has a much poorer showing. Indeed, among the industrialized nations of Europe and North America, Canada has one of the worst records on income equality, with only the U.S. scoring worse. In other words, the rich have a larger share of the national pie in Canada and in the U.S. than they do in European countries.

**CHART 5 – Income Inequality**

Income inequality is calculated by identifying the share of the national income received by the top 20 per cent of the population, and that received by the bottom 20 per cent of the population, and then establishing a ratio of the top to the bottom. (A higher number indicates a greater concentration of income among the rich, or a higher degree of inequality.)

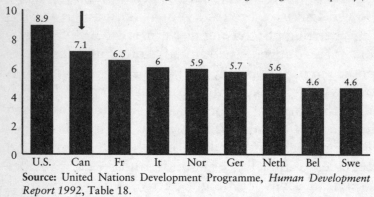

**Source:** United Nations Development Programme, *Human Development Report 1992*, Table 18.

The UN also includes another ranking to measure equality between the sexes. This "gender-sensitive" chart measures the gap between men and women in the areas of health, education, employment and wage levels. Once again, the Canadian performance here is not so impressive.

As the UN report notes: "Many countries fall in their rank in the HDI [Human Development Index] when gender sensitivity is introduced. Canada, for example, no longer occupies the top spot, but slips to number eight . . . because women have significantly lower employment and wage rates than men . . . Sweden, by contrast, moves from number 5 to number one, as it has greater equality between men and women."

Not surprisingly, the Mulroney government didn't think this information was important enough to bother us with during Canada's first-ever World Series.

With the defeat of the Mulroney government's constitutional package — the same week as the Blue Jays' victory — Ottawa finally turned its attention to the economy. But the measures it introduced late in the fall of 1992 — more spending cuts, particularly in the unemployment insurance system — left many Canadians longing for the good old days when Mulroney spent all his time on the constitution.

By cutting unemployment benefit levels and tightening eligibility requirements, the government sent a strong signal that in the last year of its mandate it intended to keep firmly to the plan it had established at the outset. That plan, which the Mulroney government outlined shortly after taking office in the fall of 1984, was to loosen the social safety net beneath Canadians and force them to adapt to the dictates of the private marketplace.

The central thrust of the strategy, as outlined only two months after its first election in a report called *A New Direction for Canada: An Agenda for Economic Renewal*, was a reduction in the role of government and a transfer of power to the private marketplace. The report was full of invective against government and the large role that government had played. Thus we were told bluntly: "Government has become too big. It intrudes too much into the marketplace and inhibits or distorts the entrepreneurial process." Government was painted throughout the report as a negative, meddlesome force; it was referred to as "expansive, intrusive government," that had created "excessive regulation and intervention." The first policy objective listed in the conclusion was to "downsize government."

One of the key parts of government that the Conservatives wanted "downsized" was the social welfare system. Indeed, much of the impetus for downsizing was a desire to weaken the scope of the welfare state, and therefore to limit its power to redistribute resources. The Conservatives, and the business interests that supported them so well financially, wanted the marketplace to play a stronger role in making decisions and allocating resources — a change which would deliver more power and more of the nation's resources to business.

Business interests have long been concerned about the power of the welfare state to interfere with the market's distribution of income. These concerns were reflected in the influential 1985 report of the Royal Commission on the Economic Union and Development Prospects for Canada, headed by former Liberal finance minister Donald Macdonald. The Macdonald report noted that the democratic process allowed citizens to "challenge the market distribution of power and income; they use the state to impose criteria of equity which modify market outcomes. The result is the welfare state, an embodiment of concepts of sharing which subordinates market results." In other words, the welfare state imposes a more equal distribution of resources than the marketplace. But the Macdonald commission wasn't just noting this phenomenon, it was voicing concerns about it. The commission was clearly worried that the welfare state was imposing a more egalitarian agenda. The commission, although set up by the Liberals, shared the new Conservative government's desire to enhance the power of the marketplace.

Thus, the report went on to suggest that perhaps the welfare state had gained too much power in recent decades at the expense of the private marketplace. "[W]e believe that in several areas, the present division of labour between state and market, the product of decades of incrementalism, contributes neither to our economy nor to our political objectives." Certainly, in a struggle between the market and the welfare state, it was clear which side the Macdonald commission was on: it spoke of the dangers of denying "the genius of the market economy."

The Mulroney government shared this desire to reduce the scope of the welfare state and put the marketplace back in control. But it knew it would have to be careful about how it presented this to Canadians. A call for a reduction in social programs would have little appeal. So instead, *A New Direction for Canada* spoke about creating an environment which "facilitates adaptation to new market realities." This deliberately confusing jargon meant that government programs should no longer protect workers from being forced to adapt to the harsh realities of the marketplace. The report, for instance, commented that the unemployment insurance program "may create obstacles to labour market adjustment." The obstacle unemployment insurance created was the cushion it offered to workers who lost their jobs. Without that cushion, these workers would presumably be more willing to "adjust" to "new market realities"; that is, they would be willing to find new work for less pay.

From the beginning, then, the Tory government had its eye on reducing the protections offered by Canada's unemployment insurance system, and it has followed through with its plan. One of the key changes has been the withdrawal of federal funding from the unemployment insurance (UI) fund, leaving the system financed by contributions from employers and employees. By this move, the government has essentially washed its hands of responsibility for unemployment. Ottawa's departure from the UI field means it has little financial incentive to reduce unemployment, as it had in the past. "By withdrawing the government's contribution to the UI fund, this bill removes a significant impetus for the government's commitment to full employment policies," argues a brief from the Metro Toronto Social Planning Council.

Interestingly, in virtually all other industrialized nations, the government contributes to the unemployment insurance system, and government contributions automatically rise as unemployment rises. This recognizes the fact that government policies have an impact on employment trends, and it gives governments an incentive to use their policy levers to keep unemployment down. The one major industrialized nation where government does not contribute to the unemployment fund — and therefore has no direct financial stake in the country's unemployment rate — is the United States.

Ottawa's decision to relegate the unemployment problem to the private sector is particularly interesting in light of the fact that employment policies have traditionally been one of the weakest areas of the Canadian welfare state. Julia O'Connor, a sociologist at McMaster University in Hamilton, Ontario, notes that while Canadian social spending is relatively generous in areas like health and education, it is noticeably ungenerous in others, including the crucial area of job training and job creation. (Other areas where Canada has a poor record compared to other industrialized nations include social support payments to individuals and families, housing allowances and day-care services.) Indeed, federal spending on job creation has declined since 1973, despite the much higher unemployment rates in recent years. "In terms of the full employment objective, Canada is one of the least successful welfare states within the OECD," says O'Connor. This is particularly significant because, O'Connor argues, unemployment is partly a strategic choice by governments rather than an economic inevitability. Neither the U.S. nor Canada has made commitments to full employment in the postwar period, she says. Instead, they have responded to high levels of unemployment by adjusting upward the rate of employment that is considered acceptable.

Just as the whittling away of unemployment insurance has left workers more vulnerable to the harshness of the marketplace, so has the erosion of the minimum wage. In 1973, a full-time worker earning the federal minimum wage had an income above the poverty line — in fact, worth 127 per cent of the poverty line. Yet by 1991, a full-time worker earning the federal minimum wage had an income well below the poverty line — indeed, only 56 per cent, or slightly more than half the poverty line, according to calculations done by the social planning council.

This erosion, although particularly acute at the federal level in the last decade or so, has been taking place as well with provincial minimum wages. In British Columbia, for instance, a full-time worker earning the provincial minimum wage earned only 70 per cent of the poverty line in 1991, compared to 150 per cent in 1973; in Ontario, the same worker earned 75 per cent of the poverty line in 1991, compared to 120 per cent in 1973. Clearly, the minimum wage is no longer the guarantee against poverty that it once was. As the social planning council notes, this is a significant change from the early part of the century, when minimum wages were enacted across the country with the explicit intention of ensuring that a working wage was "adequate to furnish the necessary cost of living."

Thus, both our unemployment and minimum wage policies are increasingly abandoning the worker to the vagaries of the marketplace. As full-time, high-paying jobs have disappeared in recent years, workers have been obliged to accept what's out there — increasingly, the lower-wage, part-time jobs of the service sector. There are now nearly 3 million Canadians supporting themselves on incomes from part-time or temporary jobs which generally pay significantly less than full-time work and offer fewer benefits, according to a 1992 Statistics Canada study called *Quality of Work in the Service Sector*.

Ottawa's move to free trade has also been an effective lever in its efforts to roll back the welfare state and force Canadians to accept the harsher reality of the marketplace. During the bitter 1988 federal election campaign, the Mulroney government insisted that the Free Trade Agreement with the United States would not affect Canada's social programs. But while the agreement does not specifically deal with social programs, it has had the effect of increasing pressure to cut them back. It has thrown open our border to goods produced by companies paying lower taxes and lower wages, thereby increasing the determination of Canadian companies to bring down Canadian taxes and wage rates. Lower taxes of course diminish our ability to pay for social programs. And so our competition with low-tax countries has become a powerful argument for those — like economist Thomas Courchene — who wish to roll back the welfare state.

Courchene makes the point that the Canadian welfare state is based on an east-west system of taxes and transfer payments and that this "does not square well with north-south economic integration.... The political economy underpinnings of the regional transfer system are likely to undergo considerable erosion." For Courchene, this is a positive development; he wants to see our welfare state dramatically overhauled and reduced in scope.

The pressure on the Canadian welfare state will only increase, of course, once Mexico is also included in the North American trading bloc. Wage rates in Mexico — roughly 98 cents an hour in Mexico's booming manufacturing area known as the "maquiladoras" — are dramatically lower than even those in the southern U.S. Furthermore, Mexican tax rates are extremely low, reflecting the virtually non-existent Mexican welfare state. It is hard to imagine how Canada would be able to finance a healthy, generous welfare state when it is in open-market competition with two countries that pay lower taxes to finance welfare systems that are comparatively small — or, in the case of Mexico, downright microscopic.

The scope of the problem can best be seen by comparing the social security benefits — including pensions, unemployment insurance and family benefits — available in the three countries. According to data compiled by the UN-affiliated International Labour Office in Geneva, Canada pays its citizens an average of $2,119 (US) a year in social security benefits. (This is less than France which has average annual benefits of $3,829 (US) or Sweden, with $4,907.) But Canada is more generous than the U.S., which pays an average benefit of $2,088 (US) a year. The gap between Canada and the U.S. is minor, however, compared to the gap of both countries *vis-à-vis* Mexico. Indeed, Mexico pays its citizens an average of only $21 (US) a year in social security benefits — *one hundred times* less than the average Canadian benefit. If one were trying to think of a way to bring pressure on the Canadian welfare state, it would be hard to come up with a better tactic than entering into a free trade deal with Mexico.

Making the safety net less secure for Canadians has not been popular. Canadians are attached to their social programs. The welfare-bashing that has worked so well in the U.S. has not been particularly effective here. Thus, the Conservative government has always voiced support for social programs, while lamenting that they are simply no longer affordable in their existing form.

But while publicly proclaiming support for Canada's social programs, Ottawa has altered and eroded them considerably. The most drastic cutting has taken place in health and post-secondary education. Between 1986 and 1991, the Mulroney government made a number of changes so that federal payments to the provinces to cover costs in these crucial areas would not keep pace with inflation and economic growth. The cumulative effects of these changes over time are simply staggering. By the year 1999–2000, the federal government will have spent $97.6 billion less on health and post-secondary education than it would have under the old federal–provincial arrangement, according to calculations done by the National Council of Welfare, a federally appointed advisory body.

Under the new scheme, federal payments in these areas will disappear at some point over the next dozen years. The national council estimates the federal payments will effectively end by 2006; other analysts, using different assumptions about economic growth, put the end earlier. Health policy consultant Michael Rachlis estimates the end will come in 2002. "Whatever the assumptions, the end result is the same . . . Sooner or later, the cash will run out," warned the national council in a 1991 brief.

This has drastically limited Ottawa's ability to enforce uniform standards and universal access across the country. It has also sent the provinces scrambling to come up with funds to keep hospitals, colleges and universities functioning, greatly contributing to the sense among Canadians that we can no long afford our social programs.

The Mulroney government has also cut back spending on welfare payments, making a mockery of its claim that it is redirecting resources to the most needy Canadians. (Indeed, 37 per cent of welfare recipients are children, according to the national council.) In the past, Ottawa had paid half the welfare bill, with provinces and municipalities making up the rest. That meant that if welfare costs rose, Ottawa's share of the costs rose. But in 1990, the Mulroney government decided to put limits on how much it would spend on welfare in the so-called "rich" provinces of Ontario, Alberta and British Columbia. As a result of budget changes, Ottawa will reduce its spending on welfare by $2 billion in the first four years of the 1990s, leaving the three provinces and their municipalities desperately short of funds just as welfare costs are rising.

And in the area of child benefits, the Mulroney government has introduced a number of changes that have greatly reduced its spending. Between 1986 and 1991, benefits were reduced by $3.5 billion, according to Ken Battle, former head of the national council, and now president of the privately funded Caledon Institute of Social Policy.

Knowing cuts are unpopular, Ottawa has tried its best to prevent Canadians from seeing what it is doing. To this end, it has carried out much of its welfare state erosion through complex, obscure changes that few Canadians understand. Moreover, Ottawa has accompanied these changes with misleading statements assuring Canadians that the changes actually strengthen social protections, when the very opposite is true. Battle, who has been a close observer of the whole process, calls the Tory strategy "social policy by stealth."

"It relies heavily on technical amendments to taxes and transfers that are as difficult to explain as they are to understand and thus largely escape media scrutiny and public attention," explains Battle. "It camouflages regressive changes in the rhetoric of equity in an attempt to convince Canadians that tax increases are tax cuts and that benefit cuts are benefit increases."

One of the best illustrations of this "stealthy" approach has been the Mulroney government's pattern of cutting back social benefits by reducing their indexation, thereby allowing the value of the benefit to be eroded over time through inflation. This method has the advantage of arousing little public attention. Not only is it highly technical and therefore dull, but its impact is hard to see; rather than happening all at once, the benefit erosions happen slowly over time.

It is not surprising then that "de-indexation" has been the cutback method of choice of the Conservative government. Former finance minister Michael Wilson used it in the government's first major assault on social welfare benefits — its attempt to reduce pension benefits for seniors in its May 1985 budget. Although that initiative failed when the Canadian public finally caught on several weeks later and seniors' groups forcefully expressed their outrage, it almost succeeded because nobody — including the dozens of press people scrutinizing the budget — noticed it at first.

While public outrage forced Ottawa to back down that time, the government has successfully used the same de-indexation method to reduce benefits in many other areas. Indeed, in 1989 it tried again and this time succeeded in reducing seniors' benefits through a trickier form of de-indexation, to which we will return later. Similarly, when Ottawa created a special tax credit to compensate low-income people for the GST, it only partially indexed the credit, so that the credit's value is eroded over time. As a result, the only Canadians who will pay more GST each year are the poorest Canadians.

Let's just look briefly at how all this works in practice. In February 1992, Ottawa announced its reforms to the child-benefits system, insisting that its new package was a major improvement. Finance Minister Don Mazankowski boasted that two-thirds of all families would receive bigger benefits as a result of the changes. And at first glance, this seemed to be the case. Under the new scheme, for instance, a family of four with an income from employment of only $20,000 a year would receive an additional $500 a year in child benefits. Although it wasn't enough, it did sound like an improvement.

But while all this was true, there was a hidden component that rendered these apparent improvements a mirage. The extra benefit will disappear like the sands of time because it is only partially indexed to inflation. Let's stop right there. Here we are, in the middle of an image comparing child benefits to disappearing sand, when we must stop and deal with a very technically complicated notion like "partial de-indexation." If I stop to explain how this works, the reader will become hopelessly bored — which, I suppose, is just what the government intended! So instead of going into details* let's just keep focused on the main point — that the value of the benefits will erode over time through inflation.

Let's return now to our $20,000-a-year family of four. Under the old system, it would have received $2,253 in child benefits in 1993. Under the new system, it receives an extra $500, bringing its new benefit total to $2,753. But look what happens in seven years (using inflation estimates from the Department of Finance): the value of the family's child benefit is reduced to a mere $2,002 (in constant 1993 dollars) according to calculations done by the Caledon

---

* Under partial de-indexation, benefit levels are indexed only to inflation above 3 per cent. Therefore, as long as inflation runs at or above 3 per cent a year, the value of the benefit is automatically eroded by 3 per cent a year.

Institute of Social Policy. Not only has the $500 bonus disappeared entirely, but the family is actually receiving less in child benefits than it would have received under the old system in 1993. In other words, the same family is actually worse off by the year 2000 than it is now — all because of the invisible hand of de-indexation. When its full impact is seen like this, de-indexation is anything but dull.

For the family of four living on welfare, the picture is even bleaker. These people are not entitled to any increase under the government's new scheme, even though they are clearly among the poorest and most vulnerable members of society. Under the government's new system they are punished, in effect, for not working. The new $500 bonus only goes to poor people who work. Single mothers who stay home to take care of their children, for instance, do not qualify for the bonus, no matter how great their needs may be, or how much they would like to work if they could find affordable day care.

So, for instance, the four-person welfare family would have received $2,253 in child benefits under the old system, and continues to receive the same amount under the new system. In seven years, however, this welfare family's child benefits will only be worth $1,861 (in constant 1993 dollars) — even though it's unlikely that the needs of those children will be any less.

All this makes a mockery of Ottawa's claim that it is directing resources more effectively to the poor. As we've just seen, the modest increase that the working poor will receive under Ottawa's new plan will more than disappear by the end of the decade, leaving these families worse off than they are now. For the poorest of the poor, there is no increase at all; and by the end of the decade, these highly vulnerable families will be considerably worse off.

Furthermore, the government's claim to be redirecting scarce resources to the poor doesn't square with another change in the new child benefit package — an increase in the child-care expense deduction. This deduction mostly benefits more affluent families, who can either afford to hire a live-in "nanny" or use a licensed day-care centre which provides receipts (as opposed to the cheaper unlicensed arrangements many lower-income parents are obliged to use). Yet despite scarce resources, Ottawa somehow found an extra $135 million to make this tax break more generous. At least some of the scarce resources the government claims to be redirecting to the poor seem to have ended up in the hands of the rich.

One of the truly clever aspects of Ottawa's "de-indexation" strategy is that it is almost impossible to see how dramatic the changes are over time. Even people who manage to resist the temptation to doze off at the first mention of "partial de-indexation" may have trouble paying attention long enough to see its full impact. The notion of a slight erosion of benefits through inflation sounds trivial, almost nit-picking.

It is only when one uses a computer model that one can see how significantly the changes will alter Canadian society.

Deep inside the federal bureaucracy this very research has taken place — although it is one of the best-kept secrets in Ottawa. The work has been done by Michael Wolfson, an economist and mathematician, who is director general of the analytical studies branch of Statistics Canada, and Brian Murphy, a senior research analyst at the branch. Together they drew up a series of computer scenarios that, among other things, show the likely long-range impact of the Conservative government's changes, including the de-indexation of both the social welfare system and the tax system.

Their findings, released in a dull academic journal called *Statistical Journal of the United Nations Economic Commission for Europe*, indicate that the changes, if left unchecked, will make Canada a much more unequal society. By the year 2036, for instance, Wolfson and Murphy found there will be an increase in the number of rich families, particularly those in the top income group. At the same time, there will be "a significant decline in the middle class." And, most disturbingly, there will be a "doubling of the 'poor.'"

The picture becomes more dramatic still in the case of the elderly. To understand this, it is necessary to know that, although the Mulroney government failed in its attempt to de-index the old age pension in 1985, it succeeded four years later in a more subtle de-indexation attempt affecting the elderly. It introduced something known as the "clawback," which meant that those with incomes above a certain level would lose part of their old-age pension. When it introduced the clawback in the 1989 budget, Ottawa made it sound as if it was taking funds exclusively from the rich. The government repeatedly described what it was doing as taking benefits away from "higher-income" Canadians. And, it was true that the cut-off point for the clawback, above which people started losing benefits, was initially fairly high — $50,000. But, once again, this cut-off point was not fully indexed to inflation. So, as time goes on, more and more people will find themselves losing benefits.

As a result, Wolfson and Murphy project that the number of old people with a middle-class standard of living will decline by about one-third, with most of these people dropping into poverty. Indeed, there will be a dramatic increase in poverty among the elderly. Wolfson and Murphy projected that by 2036, there will be *more than six times the number of elderly Canadians living in poverty*. This means that after decades of improvements in the lot of the elderly — one of the most basic goals of the postwar drive to strengthen the social safety net — Canada will once again have large numbers of old people living in poverty. Indeed, in the scenario projected by Wolfson and Murphy, almost one in four old people will be poor. The Conservative government's attempt to portray its actions as only hitting the rich could not have been more misleading.

But, except for regular readers of the *Statistical Journal of the United Nations Economic Commission for Europe*, few Canadians have any idea of what's to come.

If poverty among the elderly threatens to become once again a major social problem in Canada, one of the most pressing problems right now is female poverty — that is, poverty among women living without men. One obvious approach to begin to tackle this problem would be to bring in a national day-care program, which would allow single mothers to work rather than remaining caught in the trap of welfare. Such a solution would not only help these women and their families, it would actually fit with the conservative philosophy, with its emphasis on the work ethic and the importance of individual self-reliance.

So perhaps it was not surprising when the Mulroney government promised a national day-care program as part of its 1988 election campaign. Yet in early 1992, it abruptly announced it was shelving all such plans, on the grounds that Canadians no longer considered day care a priority. In the next chapter, we'll see just how the government came to have this insight into the hearts and minds of Canadians.

# 6

# DAY CARE OR
# THE BUSINESS LUNCH?

Years of being labelled the cronies of big business had perhaps gotten under the skin of those in the Mulroney government. This time, they decided, it was going to be different. This time they would consult the people. So Ottawa decided to turn to typical Canadians to help figure out how to deal with Canada's most pressing social problem: child poverty. A series of "focus groups" were set up to offer advice on how to best spend Ottawa's limited resources. These groups of ordinary Canadians were asked to rank the importance of a number of problems relating to children — including poverty, physical abuse, sexual abuse and day care.

The results were conclusive: the focus groups all overwhelmingly ranked poverty and abuse well above day care. Not surprisingly, everyone seemed to feel that helping hungry, battered children was more important than "babysitting." So the government, citing the results of this "consultation" with the public, announced in February 1992 that it was killing its plan for a national day-care program.

But is it reasonable to conclude from this exercise that Canadians don't care about a national day-care program? Clearly, the groups were never given any real choices. They were never asked to rank the importance of day care versus, for instance, the business entertainment deduction. Perhaps Canadians would have preferred to spend their limited resources on day care rather than squandering it on this generous tax break, which allows business executives to deduct the cost of meals, drinks and sports tickets — even private boxes at the SkyDome — at a cost to the federal treasury of more than $1 billion a year in lost revenue. That could pay for a lot of day-care centres. (Indeed, the National Council of Welfare estimates that it would cost $1.5 billion in capital spending to create day-care spaces for the 750,000 Canadian children who currently need them.)

There are in fact tax breaks worth some $8 billion a year that we could do without, according to tax professor Neil Brooks of Osgoode Hall Law School. They range from the ludicrous one mentioned above to special tax breaks for developers or for corporations to invest abroad (how does that help us?), to the special low tax rate on capital gains. Any attempt to remove any of these measures would produce howls of protest from those who benefit from them. My point is not to enter into a debate here about whether we should scrap these various measures, but to show that if the government were serious about trying to determine the priorities of Canadians, it would put some real choices on the table. What about the $4 billion Ottawa is spending on military helicopters? Do Canadians feel that's a priority? One suspects that the government never asks Canadians to give a real ranking of their priorities because it fears the results wouldn't fit with the government's plans. Imagine, for instance, a group of randomly selected Canadians being asked to rank the importance to their lives of: the business entertainment deduction, military helicopters, child care, a tax break for business to invest overseas, special tax breaks for developers, etc.

Indeed, Ottawa's decision to consult with "focus groups" — a practice popular in U.S. political and marketing circles — is particularly bizarre since the government had already spent years consulting with the public on the subject of day care. Back in 1986, a special parliamentary committee on child care heard from almost one thousand different groups across the country, as well as child-care experts and just ordinary parents who had views on the subject. The overwhelming thrust of the advice the committee received was that there was a real need for more day care, and that it should be accessible to all, affordable and run on a non-profit basis.

This was apparently not what the government wanted to hear. Indeed, it went ahead and proposed a new day-care law that would do almost exactly the opposite of what Canadians had requested. The proposed law, Bill C-144, would have done nothing to increase accessibility or affordability, and it would have made more federal funding available to private day-care operators. It also would have imposed limits on federal funding for day care. The proposals were so far from what Canadians had asked for that there was a flood of protests from child-welfare activists and day-care groups. Particularly worrisome was the notion that some of the federal funding was going to end up as profit in the hands of private day-care operators. A brief from the University of Toronto's Childcare Resource and Research Unit expressed concern that the new bill would draw "not only new Canadian entrepreneurs into child care but will encourage American businesses with substantial venture capital to enter the Canadian market."

The bill prompted a whole new round of consultations and hearings and a report by a Senate committee before Ottawa finally retreated in the face of massive opposition. But, after all this endless consultation, it is inconceivable that Ottawa still had so little notion of what Canadians thought about day care that it had to turn to "focus groups" to clarify the situation. Indeed, it is difficult to avoid the conclusion that the focus groups were little more than a cynical attempt to provide an appearance of public support for a decision that the government had already made.

And so it was that the Mulroney government abandoned its promise for a national day-care program, leaving day care in Canada an underfunded program administered through the welfare system. At the same time, Ottawa killed the universal Family Allowance program and replaced it with a targeted program. These changes have vital implications for social welfare in Canada and put us more firmly on the path towards a U.S.-style social welfare system.

Like the United States, Canada's most dramatic and growing social problem is child poverty, particularly the poverty of children in single-parent families. The lack of universal child benefits and affordable day care are major contributors to the problem. The Europeans have done a much better job in tackling child poverty, and experts in the child-welfare area argue that lower European poverty rates are partly a reflection of the better European social policies regarding children. Certainly, comprehensive day-care programs which allow single mothers to work offer a chance for these families to escape the demoralizing trap of welfare dependence.

But despite the much greater European success in the area of child poverty, the Mulroney government has looked to the U.S. rather than to Europe in developing a child-care and child-benefits package. Looking to the U.S. for guidance in fighting child poverty is roughly equivalent to looking to South Africa for guidance in how to achieve racial equality.

In many ways, the sprawling suburban region of Peel just west of Toronto seems to represent the future. Only three decades ago, most of it was farmland. But the growth of Toronto spilled over, turning much of the area into suburban sprawl, with wide-set roadways, shopping malls and seemingly endless developments of neat, new homes on fenced lots with skimpy trees.

Peel has a definite middle-class feel about it. There are pockets of affluence, as well as low-income highrises. But mostly it's a series of new communities of middle-class families who made the decision to spend an extra hour a day commuting on congested highways in order to get a bigger house and a larger lawn for their children.

But while the houses and yards seem well maintained in Peel, the public school system is in bad shape — an omen perhaps of what lies ahead for other regions. The public school system is particularly strained in Peel because of the area's rapid growth, but its problems of coping with reduced government funding are not unique. Indeed, the situation in Peel may give us cause for alarm when we remember the severe problems that have developed in the U.S. school system through underfunding. Although the situation in Canada at this point is far removed from that of the U.S., we can see in Peel the same sorts of problems taking root. Specifically, we can see how cutbacks in funding have much greater impact on the less well-to-do.

Like other school districts, Peel has seen a rapid erosion of provincial funding for its schools since the early '70s, and particularly since the early '80s. Whereas the province paid 60 per cent of its costs fifteen years ago, it now pays only 14 per cent of those costs, forcing the board to rely more and more on local municipal taxes. This has resulted in a lack of funds to build new facilities; Peel's 173 elementary and secondary schools now have a total of 600 portable classrooms to accommodate students who cannot be fitted into existing school buildings.

Last year the province cut another $20 million from the school board's $658 million budget — even as the student body grew by 3,000. The board responded by laying off 595 teachers and staff, and tightening everything from school library programs to textbook purchases. Without enough books to go around, pupils often must borrow textbooks from the library to study for a test — that is, if the library is open and there are enough copies to go around. The board also eliminated bus service which in the past transported pupils to special classes in art and music. The classes will continue, but from now on, parents must find ways to transport their children themselves.

The board also eliminated programs to teach English to immigrant children at the primary grade level — which poses particular problems in the Malton district of Peel, near Toronto's main airport, where there is a high concentration of recent immigrants and refugees. Peel trustee Laurie Cashmore says that in some Malton schools there are now primary classes (up to Grade Three) where up to 90 per cent of the pupils do not speak or understand English — the language the teacher is instructing them in.

The cutbacks have also meant less janitorial service. This may sound unimportant compared to books and language training, but it does influence the atmosphere in the schools. Cashmore notes that the board does not have the funds to hire an additional janitor if one is absent from work. If the janitor is away for a few days, she says that school washrooms and classrooms can become "filthy" — hardly an atmosphere for instilling in children a sense of community values and a respect for the environment. Similarly, a reduction in lunchroom supervision means that pupils now have to eat lunch sitting on the floor of the auditorium, where one supervisor watches over sixty of them at a time.

Cashmore sees the cuts as an assault on the public education system, and worries that things are going to get worse. She is disturbed by a phenomenon that has become common in the United States — ratepayers' groups demanding cutbacks in school spending to keep property taxes down. Cashmore says that ratepayers' groups, particularly in the more affluent sections of Peel, have launched aggressive campaigns to pare back school budgets. For instance, the Meadow Wood Rattray Residents' Association, which respresents a well-to-do enclave in Peel, suggested saving money by increasing class sizes, and noted that schools in Korea and Japan have fifty to sixty pupils in a class. The residents' association also proposed dealing with the need for more schools by renting vacant office or retail space.

It is hard to imagine that parents would choose to revamp the schools in this way, placing their children in classes of sixty pupils, located in empty retail space with inadequate recreation areas, library service and sanitation. Perhaps the simple answer is that few parents probably would be willing to do such things to schools that their own children attended. Indeed, a large number of those pushing for radical budget cuts in the public school system already send their children to private schools, according to Cashmore.

This again raises a vital aspect of the erosion of our social welfare systems — it hits some Canadians harder than others. For those who have the option of private schools, the deterioration of our public school system may not seem to be such an acute problem. Education would still continue in the public schools, but it would increasingly be a no-frills, bare-bones experience. Certainly, going to school wouldn't be as pleasant as it used to be. The surroundings would be a little cruder, a little meaner, and consequently, a child's first real experience with the world beyond home would be just a little less generous and less welcoming. Those who wanted more (and could afford more) would be free to pay extra and find it in schools outside the system.

Even for those who stay within the public system, the cutbacks are likely to hurt some more than others. For instance, Peel's decision to abolish English training for non-English speaking children in the first three grades obviously has no impact on a child who has grown up speaking English. But it has an absolutely dramatic impact on newly arrived immigrant and refugee children, who are also generally from poor families. The removal of this service for these children in Peel may turn out to be nothing short of devastating, if they become alienated from the school system at an early age because they have trouble understanding what is happening in class. The fact that there are so many of them concentrated in classes together only compounds the problem, making it less likely that they will be able to pick up English simply by hearing it spoken around them. Rather it is likely that they will become isolated in their own communities and have trouble adapting to the school system, and perhaps to Canada.

Another highly vulnerable group — the disabled — narrowly missed losing services in the broad sweep of cuts by the Peel board last year. Under provincial law, the disabled have the right to be educated in the public system. Coping with the educational needs of children with serious mental or physical disabilities clearly imposes significant costs on the system. Indeed, children with extreme handicaps often require teaching assistants on a one-to-one basis. Last year, the Peel School Board came very close to cutting back the hours of teaching assistants, including those who help the disabled.

Instead, the board froze the number of assistants — a move that already appears to be causing problems. Cashmore says that in one school's kindergarten last

September there were four children with severe disabilities, including cerebral palsy, spina bifida and autism. Despite the considerable needs of the four children, the board only supplied one teaching assistant to help out. After considerable pressure, a second assistant was added.

Cashmore fears that the proposal to cut back teaching assistants' hours will be on the table again this year. With the high costs involved, special assistance for the disabled is clearly an item that cost-conscious board members will continue to eye with great interest. And yet it is hard to imagine a more vulnerable group, and one more in need of assistance in the school system.

Indeed, the plight of the disabled illustrates the importance of a strong public school system. The costs involved in educating a mentally or physically disabled person would be out of the range of most Canadian families. And yet by pooling our resources into a public system and sharing these expenses, the cost becomes easily manageable for us as a society — and the child is ensured of an education.

Even cutbacks that would affect all students — such as the cancellation of bus service to art and music classes and the need to share textbooks — will almost certainly have less impact on children from more affluent families. Such children are likely to have access to private music and art lessons anyway, and their parents are undoubtedly willing to buy them their own textbooks. Reductions in library service are also probably less of a problem for children who have encyclopaedia sets at home, not to mention parents who have university educations.

But our public education system was supposed to try to minimize the advantages and disadvantages of birth, by placing all children together and providing them all with excellent facilities and opportunities to develop their abilities to the maximum. No public system can remove the advantages of being born into a well-to-do family, where education is encouraged and children are exposed to a wide range of cultural opportunities. But a well-funded school system, where good facilities and teaching are available to all, can go a long way towards correcting the imbalance. Indeed, the Conservative government's constant claim that the federal deficit is a terrible legacy to leave our children ignores a far more worrisome development — that our social spending cuts will leave our children with an impoverished education system that no longer even tries to give all an equal chance in life.

In a sense, notions of equality have become so deeply ingrained in Canadians that they have perhaps become part of our national psyche. This, at least, might explain an interesting phenomenon noted by James L. Whyte, who has taught economics at Georgian College in Barrie, Ontario, for the past twenty years.

131

Early in each semester, Whyte presents his class with a problem to solve. The problem boils down to this: A medical school receives far more applications than it can accept. All applicants meet the academic requirements and all have sent cheques to cover tuition fees. How does the school determine who to accept?

Whyte's students generally propose a wide range of solutions — such as selecting applicants on a first-come-first-served basis, selecting them by lottery or by the excellence of their academic credentials. One solution that is consistently unpopular and frequently absent altogether is the "price solution" — that is, raising the medical school's tuition fee. Whyte notes that when he presented this alternative to a recent class, the students reacted with hostility, rejecting it as "unfair" on the grounds that "only the children of the rich could become doctors."

When Whyte described this phenomenon recently in an article in *The Globe and Mail*, the newspaper's headline writers attributed the students' behaviour to an "alarmingly bureaucratic mindset." But why does an unwillingness to accept inequality amount to a bureaucratic mindset? Indeed, it tells us little about their attitude towards bureaucracy. But it does tell us a great deal about their attitude towards inequality.

Raising tuition fees is the way the private marketplace would solve the problem. With higher fees, students who could not afford the higher cost would simply drop out of the race, thereby reducing the number of contenders. But raising tuition fees clearly creates the potential for inequality, with competition for space largely restricted to the children of the rich or those lucky enough to find well-paying part-time jobs. As Whyte notes, year after year the assortment of young Canadians who make up his classes simply reject this solution as unfair.

Whyte's observation offers an interesting insight perhaps into Canadians and their values. It suggests that Canadians have a strong dislike of inequality.

It should be stated clearly right here that Canada is by no means an equal society. The gap between the rich and the poor is immense, and always has been. The rich élite clearly wields far more power than its numbers warrant, as a result of its prominent role in funding political parties, its ownership of the media and its control over corporations and capital.

But, in spite of these inequalities, the principle of equality has strong appeal to Canadians and is deeply embedded in some of our key social welfare programs, most notably health and education.

Canadians, for instance, have little tolerance for systems that give the rich access to better medical care. Doctors in Ontario found this out in 1986 when they went on strike over the right to "extra-bill" their patients — that is, to charge a fee above the government's medicare rate. The doctors argued that everyone would still have access to medical care, even if doctors were allowed to charge extra fees for patients willing to pay them. The Ontario government countered that extra-billing threatened to create a two-tiered system, with better medical care available only to the affluent. To the surprise of the doctors, the public sided strongly with the government. After a long and bitter strike, the demoralized doctors gave up and went back to work. And David Peterson's Liberal government, which had taken a strong stand against the doctors, won a landslide victory in the next provincial election.

The doctors' strike and the political fight that developed around it nicely captures one of the key differences between Canada and the United States — the importance attached to equality. Throughout the strike, doctors kept emergency wards operating and made a point of reassuring the public that no one would go without needed medical care. Still, the doctors failed to win much public sympathy because Ontario residents had been persuaded that extra-billing opened up the possibility of a two-tiered health-care system, with better care for those with money.

And yet in the U.S., as we've seen, Americans have learned to live with a two-tiered system. Indeed, for many Americans without financial resources, access to medical care can be difficult to attain. Although hospitals — public and private — are legally bound to treat emergency cases arriving at the hospital in need of urgent care, some hospitals have gotten around this by, for instance, closing their trauma units. Canadian journalist Jamie Swift interviewed a

Los Angeles doctor who told him that in crowded public hosptials, doctors sometimes refer to uninsured patients as cases of AMF/YO-YO — "Adios, motherfucker. You're on your own." And indeed these people are on their own: as we've seen, it's estimated that some 100,000 Americans die each year for lack of proper medical care.

This kind of gross inequality simply does not exist in Canada, because Canadians have developed more egalitarian approaches to social welfare. American commentators have often suggested that the key difference between Americans and Canadians is that Canadians are more deferential to authority, by which the commentators mean Canadians are more tolerant of big government. Americans, on the other hand, seem to be more tolerant of the unchecked power of big private interests, and more tolerant of inequality in general. Indeed, it's possible that the characteristic that most distinguishes us from Americans is not so much a tolerance for big government as a distaste for inequality.

This explains why the Mulroney government has had to tread more carefully than its U.S. counterpart in cutting back the welfare state. While Ronald Reagan built a campaign around attacks on "welfare queens," Mulroney professed that his commitment to universal social systems was a "sacred trust." And, as we've seen, the Mulroney government has tried to confuse Canadians into believing that its reforms are aimed at achieving greater equality, that it is simply redirecting help to the neediest. Interestingly, one of the few voices in Canada attacking welfare recipients has been that of prominent journalist Diane Francis, who was born and educated south of the border, in Chicago.

So instead of a head-on attack against our social welfare system and its egalitarian goals, the Conservative government has undermined the system by chipping away at its financial supports. And even here, the approach has been subtle, rather than direct. There have been no announcements of massive spending cuts or programs killed, just a gradual erosion of federal funds for health and post-secondary education through a decision to restrain the growth of transfer payments to the provinces. When Dr. Michael Rachlis mentioned on CBC Radio's *Morningside* in January 1991 that there would be no more federal payments to cover the cost of federal funding of medicare by the year 2002, host Peter Gzowski expressed surprise. If a Canadian as well informed as Gzowski is unaware of the federal government's complete withdrawal of funds from our most important social program, we might conclude that many others have also missed this development.

In some ways, this more subtle, back-door approach to social welfare erosion is more dangerous than a head-on attack. Canadians would likely reject a head-on attack, just as Ontario residents rejected the attempt by doctors to create a two-tiered system of medical care, because it offended strongly held sentiments about the importance of equal access. But with the more subtle approach of underfunding, it has been harder to see what's going on and therefore harder to resist.

In this sense, the attack has been successful. The Conservative government has been able to achieve indirectly, through underfunding, what it never would have achieved with a direct attack on the egalitarian goals of our social welfare systems. By cutting back funding, the Mulroney government has put our social systems at risk. Indeed, many Canadians now feel that these systems are in financial crisis and wonder if perhaps we simply can't afford them any more. It is to this fallacy that we now turn.

# 7

# WHY LIBRARY BOOKS ARE AS IMPORTANT AS NINTENDO: THE CASE FOR PUBLIC SPENDING

It was one of those little developments that almost passed by unnoticed: Toronto City Council decided last summer that financial pressures obliged it to slash the budgets of public libraries. After a minor ripple of concern in the media, the story quickly became lost in the welter of stories of cutbacks and restraint and budget deficits. Certainly, nobody semed to question what was happening. Here, in one of the richest countries in the world, we had convinced ourselves that we could no longer afford to provide books in our public libraries — surely one of the most basic resources for a society that would like to excel in literacy and educational achievements, not to mention the "global marketplace."

While there's enough money for Nintendo and other expensive and frivolous items of private consumption, there's a growing sense that we can no longer afford things we pay for communally through our taxes — things that, by any standard, are important items. Indeed, just about everything we pay for communally — health care, education, public parks, rail service, mail delivery, as well as benefits for the elderly, the poor, and the unemployed — are all facing the axe in one form or another. It's all part of an attitude that has held sway in government and business circles for the past decade: anything that we pay for communally is out, private consumption is in. Thus, library service is out, Nintendo is in.

The call for public spending restraint has been so loud and constant that few Canadians even question it any more. There is an air of resignation as federal and provincial governments cut back spending in all the key social welfare areas in the name of deficit reduction.

Yet, despite all the attention Canadians have devoted to the subject of government spending, there has been virtually no attention paid to a crucial fact: Canadian government spending is low by international standards. Certainly, Canadian spending is modest compared to spending by the western European countries. According to data from the OECD, Canadian government spending on all programs amounted to 35.2 per cent of its GDP in 1988, while Germany spent 45.3 per cent and France spent 47.3 per cent — reflecting the much higher social spending in these countries. The U.S., however, spent only 32.0 per cent.

Another interesting fact that receives little attention is that, as we've seen, countries with high social spending do just as well as — if not better than — countries with low social spending. This cuts to the heart of the debate about the future of the welfare state. In recent years, the conventional wisdom has been that there's a trade-off between social spending and economic growth, that too much spending on social programs hampers a country's ability to prosper and compete in the global marketplace. Economist Thomas Courchene, for instance, says that "there is a growing feeling in many quarters that the magnitude of the overall social policy network and the disincentives embodied in it contribute to Canada's inability to perform up to its economic potential." Courchene is clearly pleased to get on the bandwagon of those "in many quarters" who believe that we must pare back our social welfare spending in order to prosper economically.

But this view ignores the compelling counter-example of Europe. If the theory of Courchene and others were true, we could expect the countries of northern and western Europe, with their high spending and more generous social programs, to be an economic backwater. But of course this is not the case. As we saw in Chapter One, the high-spending European countries experienced comparatively good productivity growth over the decade of the 1980s — stronger growth indeed than the U.S. or Canada, where social spending was considerably less.

And this pattern holds true over time. In a detailed study of economic growth patterns in eighteen Western nations over the past 160 years, Swedish sociologist Walter Korpi found that there was no evidence to support the free market argument that social spending hampers economic growth. Korpi, professor of social policy at the Swedish Institute for Social Research in Stockholm, also noted that the post-1945 period, when the welfare state grew dramatically in most Western countries, was also the period of greatest economic growth.

"[I]n glaring contrast to the predictions of the market liberal hypothesis, the Golden Age of economic growth coincided with the extension of the welfare state," notes Korpi. He concluded that the universal welfare state, which is "often singled out by critics as having particularly negative consequences for economic efficiency, is not found to be associated with lower growth rates."

The example of Europe is often brushed aside by free-market enthusiasts like Courchene. In *Social Policy for the 1990s*, Courchene dismisses the European situation by saying, in an appendix, that the higher social spending in Europe is mostly due to the fact that there are proportionately more old people there. As a result, Courchene says that Europe spends more on pensions, and Canada will too when its population ages. But the situation is more complex, as we discover when we read the Macdonald royal commission report, which Courchene cites as his source. According to the commission, the fact that Canadian pension spending is relatively low is more than just a reflection of the larger proportion of old people in Europe. "Our expenditures are lower because Canadian benefits, too, are lower," writes the commission. Indeed, the commission notes that, as a proportion of GDP, Canadian spending per pensioner is "smaller than that of every other OECD country but Japan."

So it is not just that there are more old people receiving pensions in Europe, it is also that European pensions are more generous. Even if we add in Canadian government spending through the tax system on private pension plans and RRSPs, and leave out equivalent programs in Europe, the commission notes that "our nation moves up only to tenth place, still well behind European countries." Furthermore, as we saw in the last chapter, changes introduced by the Conservative government, including the clawback, will have the effect of diminishing the growth of spending on Canadian pensions in the future. A 1986 study by the International Monetary Fund found that Canada will continue over the next few decades to have the lowest public spending on pensions and other age-related social expenditures of seven major industrialized countries.

But surely the key point is that the Europeans spend considerably more on social programs than

Canada does — whether on pensions, day care, family benefits, or whatever — and yet the Europeans still experience strong economic growth. Indeed, a private Swiss organization which produces an annual World Competitiveness Report placed five European countries with large welfare states — Germany, Denmark, the Netherlands, Austria and Sweden — in the top ten in its international ranking of economic strength and competitiveness. Interestingly, three of these countries — Denmark, the Netherlands and Sweden — are known for particularly high social spending. The competitiveness report ranked Canada in eleventh place. The United States, which was in second place in 1991, dropped to fifth last year.

Courchene and others often raise the example of Japan to counter arguments about social spending. Japan has low social spending and yet ranks high in economic growth and competitiveness. But while Japan does not fit with the high-spending European model, it also doesn't fit the low-spending U.S. model. Unlike the U.S., Japan has a relatively small gap between the rich and the poor. Indeed, Japan ranks right up there with Sweden as having one of the world's most equitable income distributions. The lowest-earning 40 per cent of the Japanese population, for instance, receives 21.9 per cent of all income in Japan; in the United States, this bottom group receives only 15.7 per cent of all income; in Canada, 17.5 per cent, according to the UN Human Development Report.

Interestingly, Japan achieves this relatively equal distribution of income largely through its private marketplace, partly because of its more equal distribution of wages and partly because of its high employment levels. As a result, there is less need for the equalizing effects of social programs. In a sense, Japan manages to achieve the goal of a social welfare state — greater equality — without actually having much of a social welfare state.

Indeed, the Japanese example is instructive for Canada. Perhaps the most important feature about Japan that we should note is not its low social spending but rather its high degree of equality. Japan has accomplished a high degree of equality, as well as a high degree of economic growth and competitiveness — as have Sweden and Germany, for that matter. Perhaps the lesson for us to learn from the Japanese example is that economic equality — whether achieved through the welfare state or through the private marketplace — is a good basis for a productive economy. After all, if more citizens have money to spend, there will presumably be a greater demand for goods and services, and thus a stimulus for the economy.

If the Canadian business class were willing to distribute income more equally through the marketplace, the need for a strong social welfare system would no doubt diminish in Canada as well. Indeed, social policy consultant Leon Muszynski argues that more equality in wage levels and higher employment are as important as social programs in achieving greater equality.

Furthermore, it is noteworthy that those who are inspired by Japan's low social spending are not similarly inspired by Japan's relatively progressive tax system: Japan has high corporate taxes and a significant wealth tax. Gordon Bale, a law professor at Queen's University, notes that revenue from wealth taxes make up a larger proportion of Japan's total tax revenue than is the case in virtually any other industrialized nation. (Canada, by contrast, doesn't even have wealth taxes, such as an inheritance tax or an annual tax on net personal wealth.) And yet we hear no calls for these features of the Japanese miracle to be reproduced in Canada.

Besides, the Japanese example does nothing to refute the basic point — that high social spending can co-exist comfortably with strong economic growth, as it does in Europe. So it's useful to ask how the European countries have managed to accomplish all this: high social spending, high-level social benefits and a high level of growth. The answer will come as a surprise to many Canadians, since it flies in the face of another key piece of our conventional wisdom: that low taxes are necessary for economic growth.

Basically, European countries have managed to combine extensive social welfare with strong economic growth by paying a lot of taxes. Indeed, while Canadians complain of high taxes, our taxes are only high in comparison to the U.S. In 1989, Canadian taxes amounted to 35. 5 per cent of our GDP, compared to 38.1 per cent of GDP in Germany, 43.8 per cent in France and 56.1 per cent in Sweden. In the U.S., however, taxes accounted for only 30.1 per cent.

**CHART 6 – Taxes**
Government taxes as a per cent of GDP, 1989.

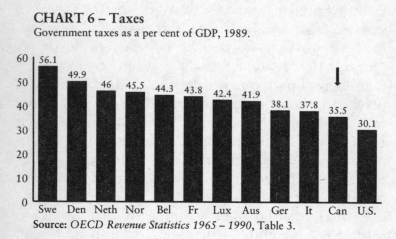

Source: *OECD Revenue Statistics 1965 – 1990*, Table 3.

Europeans enjoy greater social benefits largely because they pay for them. But — and this is the key part — this apparently hasn't harmed their economic growth. Indeed, as we've seen, their economic growth has overall been stronger than ours.

Nor have the Europeans attained their high-level social benefits simply by going into debt. Some European countries, such as Belgium, Italy and the Netherlands, had debts relatively larger than Canada in 1990. But others, including France, Germany, Denmark and even very high-spending Sweden, all had much smaller debts than Canada or the United States.

When Sweden found itself saddled with a large debt in the early '80s, it managed to reduce that debt without cutting social programs significantly. By 1990, it had one of the smallest debts in the industrialized world.

**CHART 7 – Debt**

Government gross public debt as a per cent of GDP, 1990.

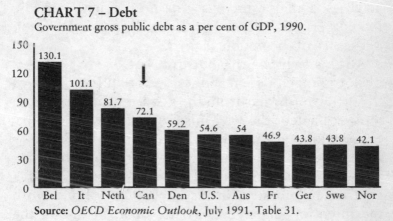

Source: *OECD Economic Outlook*, July 1991, Table 31.

As for the Canadian debt, it is less of a problem than the debt-mongers would have us believe. Contrary to the alarmist statements of business leaders and commentators, there has been a real decline in the size of the annual defict over the past decade. As tax expert Neil Brooks has shown, the deficit, as a percentage of our Gross Domestic Product, dropped from 8.7 per cent in 1984 to 4.5 per cent in 1991. This deficit reduction was accomplished through spending cuts and tax increases, and the impact of both of these on the deficit will become greater as time goes on. This will bring down the deficit, and eventually start

147

reducing the accumulated national debt as well. As Wolfson and Murphy from Statistics Canada have shown, these spending cuts and tax increases will result in massive savings to the federal government. But the savings, say Wolfson and Murphy, "come at a price — a major increase in the incidence of low income, especially among the elderly, and a reduction in the size of the middle class."

All this suggests that Ottawa has tried to accomplish too much deficit reduction too quickly. Part of the problem springs from the government's refusal to look at its debt the way businesses or even ordinary citizens look at their debts. Businesses and ordinary citizens regularly go into debt — for things that they consider important — and they pay off those debts over time. A family, for instance, buys a house with the intention of paying off the debt, including the enormous interest costs attached to that debt, over 25 years. "Nobody gets apoplectic about paying a mortgage over 25 years," says Wolfson. And businesses write off their capital expenditures on plant and equipment over time as well.

But, oddly, governments treat their spending as one-time costs that are added in a lump to the government debt, rather than amortized over time like a mortgage. Thus, all government spending — including even capital costs like building hospitals and universities — are treated in government accounts as one-time expenditures, even though the benefits of these facilities last for dozens of years. If we amortized these sorts of costs over time — as any business or private citizen would in their own accounting — the federal deficit would drop significantly.

Instead, however, Ottawa has created a near-hysteria in the land over the deficit. It has told us, for instance, that we spend 36 cents of every tax dollar to pay off the national debt, while Japan spends only 20 cents of its tax dollar on such debt-servicing costs. Many Canadians are now convinced that if we do not get our deficit under control, we will seriously hamper our ability to compete in the world. But they might be less worried if Ottawa pointed out, as *Toronto Star* columnist Thomas Walkom has, that, when all levels of government are taken into consideration, Canada's debt-servicing costs (as a percentage of tax revenue) are roughly similar to Japan's — and yet Japan continues to prance proudly on the stage of international competition.

But Ottawa apparently has no interest in pointing this out. The reason may be that the deficit is a useful vehicle for arguing that government spending is out of control and must be curbed, which seems to be the ultimate goal of the Conservatives. Indeed, the Conservative government has, from the beginning, used the deficit to illustrate its argument that spending grew wildly out of control under previous Liberal governments in the '70s, and that the only responsible course now is to significantly reduce that spending.

There is another way to look at the deficit problem. Rather than seeing it resulting from the growth in

149

government spending in the '70s, it is equally valid to see it as the product of reductions in tax revenues during that same decade. Indeed, a document published by the federal finance department in April 1980 shows that tax breaks introduced in budgets throughout the '70s reduced corporate, personal and sales tax revenues by more than $14 billion a year by the end of that decade. This drop in tax revenue contributed significantly to the growth of Canada's debt.

This suggests that government spending should not necessarily be seen as the villain of the deficit story. Equally responsible for our deficit plight — if we want to consider it that — is the reduction in tax revenues. Indeed, if we had followed the example of Europe and maintained higher tax revenues, our deficit situation would be dramatically different. Neil Brooks notes that if Canada had simply maintained throughout the '70s the level of taxation that it had had in 1974, our debt would have been roughly half of what it had become by the early '80s, when it started to be considered a serious problem.

The story becomes even more fascinating. Using data from the federal finance department and the OECD, Brooks has done calculations which show that if Canada had imposed the same level of taxation on Canadians as European countries imposed on their citizens throughout the last decade, Ottawa would have collected so much additional revenue that we would now have no deficit at all. In fact, we'd have a surplus of $88.5 billion! Ottawa could have devoted a good chunk of this additional revenue to social spending, as the Europeans did.

These startling facts challenge the Canadian conventional wisdom, which says that reducing government spending is the key to getting our economy in order. This popular view is based on the myth that money paid in taxes simply disappears down a big black hole somewhere, never to surface again. In fact, it is recycled back into the economy in the form of payments for services, goods or direct transfer payments to citizens.

**CHART 8 – Impact of Higher Taxes on the Deficit**

| Year | Canadian tax revenue as a % of GDP | EC* average tax revenue as a % of GDP | Canadian deficit (in billions) | Additional Canadian revenue if EC rate applied in Canada | Additional revenue with compounded interest (in billions) |
|------|------|------|------|------|------|
| 1982 | 33.5 | 38.0 | 11.9 | 16.8 | 31.56 |
| 1983 | 33.0 | 39.3 | 25.7 | 25.6 | 43.95 |
| 1984 | 33.0 | 39.4 | 31.7 | 28.5 | 44.71 |
| 1985 | 33.1 | 39.5 | 37.0 | 30.6 | 43.87 |
| 1986 | 33.7 | 40.1 | 33.9 | 32.4 | 42.45 |
| 1987 | 34.8 | 40.5 | 30.7 | 31.4 | 37.6 |
| 1988 | 34.6 | 40.6 | 27.6 | 36.3 | 39.72 |
| 1989 | 35.3 | 39.9 | 26.8 | 29.9 | 29.9 |
| Total | | | 225.3 | | 313.8 |

| | | |
|---|---|---|
| Additional revenue: | $313.8 billion | * European Community |
| Minus Canadian Deficit: | $225.3 billion | |
| Surplus: | $ 88.5 billion | |

Political scientist Gosta Esping-Andersen argues that even very high taxes don't necessarily hurt economic growth because governments simply pump the money back into the economy. "In the '30s and '40s, the big economists warned that if the welfare state grew beyond 25 to 30 per cent of the economy, there would be serious trouble. Today countries like Sweden and Denmark spend 50 per cent or more of their GDP without it seemingly affecting their economic performance," he said.

Indeed, unlike private spending, which often goes towards frivolous items of private consumption — from VCRs to jewellery to fur coats — public spending generally goes to socially useful projects that help improve a country's productivity. This includes investment in "public infrastructure" items such as highways, airports and railway systems, as well as items that improve the education and health of the workforce, like schools, universities and hospitals.

Ironically, this kind of spending may be particularly important in an era of global competition. U.S. economist Robert Reich has observed that these sorts of investments may be an especially effective way to improve a country's productivity in an age of capital mobility. Indeed, investing in business by providing more and more tax breaks may be less reliable, with capital now poised to move to more favourable locations in search of lower taxes, wages and environmental standards. By investing in our public infrastructure and in the health and education of our workforce, we can at least ensure that the benefits will stay in the country and help give us a competitive advantage.

Indeed, cutbacks in public spending in the U.S. have already caused a serious erosion in the U.S. national infrastructure, with major implications for the country's future competitiveness, according to a group of 327 economists who signed an open petition to U.S. political leaders. The petitioners, including prominent figures like John Kenneth Galbraith, Robert Heilbroner, Robert Reich and Lester Thurow, argue that there is an urgent need for $30 billion in new public investment "Higher productivity — the key to higher living standards — is a function of public, as well as private investment," the petition read. "If America is to succeed in an increasingly competitive world, we must expand efforts to equip our children with better education and our workers with more advanced skills. We must assure that disadvantaged children arrive at school age healthy and alert. . . . We must fix our bridges and expand our airports."

It could be added that smart social spending now may end up saving money later on. Children raised in poverty, with inadequate child care, education and health care may well end up costing society more in the long run if they require additional medical attention, welfare support or, for that matter, court time and prison space. It is interesting to note that the U.S., with its low social spending, also boasts an unusually large prison population. There are 426 prisoners per 100,000 Americans — a rate roughly five times as high as the rates found in western European countries, according to the UN.

Big government spending seems wasteful and costly to us largely because we suffer from what Esping-

Andersen terms "the fiscal illusion" — the notion that we save money if we buy services privately, rather than pay for them through our taxes. In fact, all we are doing is shifting the cost. Certainly, any meaningful comparison between taxes in Canada and the U.S. must include the fact that Canadians are paying for their health care when they pay their taxes. U.S. taxes are somewhat lower overall, but, as we've seen, a U.S. family may still find itself facing more than $5,000 (US) in medical insurance costs, plus thousands of dollars in additional medical expenses. To leave this out of the equation is to distort any comparison of Canadian-U.S. tax rates.

Indeed, comparisons between prices in Canada and the U.S. — often cited in articles about cross-border shopping — fail to take into consideration that U.S. bargains on some items are offset by much higher costs in other areas where Canadian subsidies or public systems create lower prices. For instance, a 1991 study by Wolfson and Murphy of Statistics Canada shows that U.S. prices are much lower on meat, dairy products, alcohol, tobacco, clothing and footwear and household equipment. But, the study found, U.S. prices were much higher on items such as housing fuel and power costs, medical and health services, education and culture and recreation. Canadians may pay more for alcohol, tobacco and dishwashers, but it costs us less to heat our houses, go to the doctor and get a good university education.

Furthermore, a system of public rather than private services may in the long run be cheaper, since there are greater economies of scale and opportunities to reduce administrative costs. This helps explain the bizarre fact that roughly one-third of Americans have inadequate health coverage even though Americans spend more per capita on health care than any country in the world. This apparent paradox can be explained almost entirely by the highly inefficient private health-care system in the U.S

Indeed, it is worth taking a closer look at this whole phenomenon, because it offers a stunning contradiction to the oft-repeated line about private enterprise always being more efficient. If we compare the private U.S. system to the public health-care system in Canada — or the public systems in any of the European countries — we see just how untrue this can be. In health care, then, we have a textbook example of the difference between the efficiency of the private and public sectors in delivering a basic service, and the results offer a sharp rebuke to those who extol the efficiencies of the marketplace.

As we've seen in earlier chapters, the evidence strongly suggests that the higher costs of running the U.S. system are not related to better health results. In virtually every measure of a nation's health — infant mortality, maternal mortality, longevity — the U.S. ranks poorly compared to Canada and Europe, obviously because so many Americans lack access to proper health care.

But, to this damning indictment, we can also add the exorbitant costs of the U.S. system. If we look at total spending on health care, the U.S. leads the pack by a country mile. According to OECD data for 1989, total spending on health care amounted to $1,683 per person in Canada, $1,232 in Germany, $1,274 in France, $1,361 in Sweden — but $2,354 in the U.S. (all in U.S. dollars). The U.S. spending was more than double the OECD average and 40 per cent higher than in Canada. Furthermore, the gap is getting bigger. "U.S. spending is the highest in the world and continutes to increase more rapidly than in virtually all other countries," George J. Schieber and Jean-Pierre Poullier, two OECD analysts, wrote in the spring 1991 issue of *Health Affairs*.

How can this be possible? A major part of the difference can be attributed to the higher administrative costs in running the U.S. system, with its 1,500 private insurance companies. In the U.S., each hospital typically must devote enormous clerical and professional time and office space — often an entire hospital floor — to the job of billing patients and collecting from insurance companies, which all offer different health plans. (Often more than one insurance company is involved, and it is necessary to assess the amount of payment covered by each insurer and that owed by the patient.) In Canada, however, where the provincial government is the only insurer, the processing of health claims is much less complicated and less labour-intensive. Of course, in addition to the more complex processing of claims in the U.S. system, there is also the fact that private insurers take a profit out of their revenues. As a result of profits and higher processing costs, administrative costs in the U.S. system amounted to between $400 and $497 (US) per person in 1987, according to a study by two U.S. doctors, Steffie Woolhandler and David Himmelstein, published in the *New England Journal of Medicine* in 1991. The equivalent costs in Canada came to just $117 to $156 (US) per person. Another study that year by the U.S. government's General Accounting Office found an even bigger discrepancy: it estimated that administrative costs were five times higher in the U.S. than in Canada.

Furthermore, the administrative costs of the U.S. system are growing dramatically, while those in Canada are falling. U.S. health bureaucracy costs rose by 37 per cent between 1983 and 1987, while Canadian administrative costs actually experienced a slight drop, according to the Woolhandler and Himmelstein study. At the present rate of growth, the study found that administration costs in the U.S. system will consume one-half of the entire U.S. health care budget by the year 2020!

Ironically, the problem has only been exacerbated by recent moves in the U.S. to curtail spiralling health costs. A whole new mini-industry of health-care cost-containment specialists has been unleashed on hospitals and doctors, in an attempt to scrutinize practices and weed out potential waste. Not only has this placed restrictions on the practice of medicine, but it has been extremely costly. "Each piece of medical terrain is meticulously inspected except that beneath the inspectors' feet," notes the study. "Paradoxically, the cost-management industry is among the fastest-growing segments of the health care economy and is expected to generate $7 billion in revenues by 1993." The authors go on to argue that all of this obscures the fact that the inefficiencies in the U.S. system are structural, and are directly related to the fact that the system is private rather than public.

"In contrast, Canada has evolved simple mechanisms to enforce an overall budget, but it allows doctors and patients wide latitude in deciding how the funds are spent," the Woolhandler and Himmelstein study concludes. "Universal comprehensive coverage under a single, publicly administered insurance program is the sine qua non of such administrative simplification." Indeed, the savings generated by a U.S. conversion to a Canadian-style system would be phenomenal. According to the authors: "Reducing our administrative costs to Canadian levels would save enough money *to fund coverage for all uninsured and underinsured Americans* [italics added]."

The situation is full of irony. The free market proponents of the U.S. system like to make the case that a public health-care system like Canada's is overly bureaucratic and rife with excessive government intervention. A 1990 editorial in *The Wall Street Journal*, for instance, described Canada's system as in danger of becoming "Soviet-like." George Bush pushed the Soviet image further still. In his acceptance speech at the Republican convention in Houston last summer, Bush denounced the idea of a public health care system: "Who wants health-care with a system with the efficiency of the House Post Office and the compassion of the KGB?" he asked.

And yet, it is the U.S. system, with its massive health-care administration and army of health-care cost inspectors that more closely resembles the bureaucratic overload conjured up by these Soviet images. For instance, the private insurer, Blue Cross/Blue Shield of Massachusetts, which provides coverage for 2.7 million subscribers, employs 6,682 workers. By contrast, British Columbia manages to administer its health-care system for more than 3 million residents with a much leaner staff — less than one-fifteenth the size — of just 435 provincial civil servants.

The U.S. health-care system reveals the disastrous consequences of leaving a vital public service to the private sector. Not only does the private system produce inequitable results, with many people being denied access to health care, but it also produces surprising inefficiencies. Amartya Sen, an economist at Harvard University, explains that while the marketplace may work well for distributing "private goods," it functions poorly for "public goods."

In the case of private goods — such as a toothbrush, a bicycle or an apple — the benefit provided by the product is really only available to the person who purchases it, and therefore a price can be set by determining how much someone is willing to pay for it. But with public goods — such as a clean environment or the absence of epidemics — the benefits are shared by all and are therefore noncompetitive. "When uses of commodities are noncompetitive (as they are in the case of public goods), the rationale for the market mechanism does not operate very well," notes Sen. With public goods, "the system of giving a good to the highest bidder does not have much merit, since one person's consumption does not exclude that of another. Instead, our *aggregate* benefits have to be compared with costs of production, and here the market mechanism functions badly."

Far from being an economic imperative, the erosion of our public systems may, in the long run, be a recipe for economic and social decline. Our obsession with cost-cutting has blinded us to the dangers of letting our systems decline, with potentially disastrous consequences for the future. Rather than viewing the cost of our social welfare as money disappearing down a black hole, we should regard it as money invested in the future.

This idea was expressed clearly in 1943 in the concluding remarks by Leonard Marsh in his *Report on Social Security for Canada:*

Finally, the obvious but vital point must be made that social security payments are not money lost. The social insurances, and even some straightforward disbursements like children's allowances, are investments in morale and health, in greater family stability, and from both material and psychological viewpoints, in human productive efficiency. They demand personal and community responsibilities; but in the eyes of most of the people who are beneficiaries, give a more evident meaning to the ideas of common effort and national solidarity. It has yet to be proved that any democracy which underwrites the social minimum for its citizens is any weaker or less wealthy for doing so.

Fifty years later, there is still no evidence to contradict this eloquent statement — just a lot of noisy rhetoric.

# 8

## As Canadian as . . . Equality

Only a few years ago it would have been political heresy to utter such a thought, but by June 1992, a prominent provincial politician seemed to have no qualms about suggesting publicly that Canada's most cherished social program may have to go. "I'm beginning to think that maintaining a universal health-care system into the next century may not be possible, unless we become filthy rich," Newfoundland Health Minister Chris Decker told *The Globe and Mail*. And Decker's comment wasn't just provincial wrangling to get more money out of Ottawa. He went on to add that he didn't think the federal government could afford to maintain the medicare system either.

Decker's remark — and the lack of protest from around the country — shows how much the Canadian political landscape has changed in the past decade. Whereas Brian Mulroney felt the need to declare universal social programs a "sacred trust" in his first national campaign eight years ago, politicians now feel comfortable publicly suggesting that even the centrepiece of our social welfare system may simply have to go. There is no evidence that Canadians are any less fond of medicare, but there is lots of evidence that we have come to accept the notion that we can no longer afford our social programs. The implication is that the welfare state is a costly drain on our resources.

The Conservative government of Brian Mulroney has been the leading proponent of this view in Canada, but the same ideas can now be found, to a greater or lesser extent, in all the major political parties and at all levels of government. Indeed, this attitude has become part of mainstream thinking in Canada in the '90s. And yet, as we have seen, this widespread belief is not based on any reliable foundation. Many of the world's advanced industrial nations have more extensive welfare states than we do — and are more than holding their own in the competitive markets of the '90s.

Perhaps the best observation on the subject comes from Walter Korpi, the Swedish professor. In his modest office at Stockholm University, Korpi shrugs when asked the key question: Can we afford the welfare state in the 1990s? Korpi has no doubt heard the question many times before, and a faint, sly smile passes over his face as he responds: "As much as we ever could."

The answer is at first disappointing. I was hoping for a resounding "Yes" from this godfather of the Swedish welfare state. But on further reflection, I see how profound Korpi's answer is. What he is really saying is that, yes, the welfare state is expensive, but it always has been. And we can afford it as much now as we ever could. And, as Korpi has demonstrated in his own studies, many countries which have paid that high price are prosperous and thriving in the international economy.

Thus the real question is not whether we can afford the welfare state. (We can.) The real question is: Do we *want* to afford it? Are we willing to pay for it? The question is not economic but political. We can afford the welfare state — if we want to.

Contrary to the prevailing North American wisdom, the welfare state is not too expensive, any more than video cameras or microwave ovens or air-conditioned cars are too expensive. It's all a question of our priorities, a question of how we want to spend our money. The notion that we must cut back our *public* expenditures is based on the questionable assumption that our *private* expenditures are somehow more important — that Nintendo is more important than library services.

But in assessing the importance of the welfare state, an interesting distinction quickly emerges — the welfare state may be more important to some than to others. And this brings us to the heart of the issue about the welfare state. Its real impact is not on a country's productivity growth but rather on the degree of equality among its citizens. Welfare states seem to create more equal societies. In many ways, the push to reduce the role of government is really an attempt to roll back some of the egalitarian gains that have accompanied the rise of the welfare state.

In the final analysis, the future of the welfare state in Canada boils down to the importance that we attach to equality.

The European countries are relatively equal societies; the gap between the rich and the poor is less pronounced than it is in the United States or Canada. And Sweden, the most advanced welfare state, has an even more egalitarian distribution of income than the other European countries. One of the most interesting ways to illustrate this is with a chart showing the size of the middle class; that is, the percentage of the population whose incomes fall within a certain defined range of the median or mid-point income.

**CHART 9 – The Size of the Middle Class**
The middle class represents families whose incomes fall between 0.625 and 1.5 times the median income. Percent of population in the middle class.

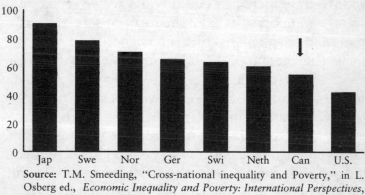

Source: T.M. Smeeding, "Cross-national inequality and Poverty," in L. Osberg ed., *Economic Inequality and Poverty: International Perspectives*, 1991, Table 2.2.

Ironically, although we tend to think of European countries as class-based societies, the truth is that the European countries today are really middle-class societies, with fewer at the upper and lower ends. Among industrialized nations, it is the United States where class divisions are most pronounced, where the middle class is relatively small and the gulf between the rich and the poor more closely resembles the gulf between the nobility and peasantry in pre-revolution France.

To begin with, the distribution of wages and earnings in the private marketplace tends to be more equal in European countries, notes U.S. economist Timothy Smeeding. Furthermore, European countries increase that equality through their more extensive social welfare programs, Smeeding says. Europeans pay higher taxes, and that money is then redistributed through social programs on a more equitable basis.

But redistributing income is only one way that the welfare state increases equality. As we've seen, many welfare state benefits take the form of services rather than cash payments. While such benefits do not show up in the income equality statistics, they have the effect of creating a more equal society, by ensuring that low-income people — as well as affluent people — have access to high-level benefits. Thus, a low-income American family not only has limited income but likely also lacks access to health care, child care and properly funded schools. A European family with equivalent income is better off, because it has access to high-level public services.

As federal and provincial governments in Canada cut back social services and leave these areas increasingly to the private sector, they risk creating greater inequality. Some neoconservative critics have argued that by applying market principles, we can increase the efficiency of our systems and save money. But, as we saw in the last chapter with the example of health care, there is little evidence of efficiency gains; certainly in the case of health care just the opposite is true. What is clear, however, is that such privatization leads to greater inequality.

That inequality can be a matter of life and death. In the U.S., lack of financial resources leaves many Americans receiving inadequate care and, in some cases, dying as a result. As Vicente Navarro puts it: "There are classes in the United States, and how people live and die depends largely on their class."

The egalitarian benefits of public health services can be seen historically in the advances of life expectancy in Britain. Amartya Sen, the Harvard economist, notes that at the beginning of every decade this century, there has been an increase in life expectancy at birth in England and Wales. The increase has been in the range of one to four years per decade. But in the case of the two war decades — the 1910s and the 1940s — the increase in life expectancy was much larger, closer to seven years (excluding war mortalities). Sen explains this by noting that in the war decades, the health of the entire civilian population improved due to wartime public health and nutrition programs that made the distribution of food and health care more equitable. "The role of the state in operations of nutritional care and health facilities can make a real difference," Sen argues, "and the contribution of these social arrangements must not be underestimated in our 'vision of society.'"

In education, too, a public system is crucial to equality. The idea of applying a private, free market approach to public education has been popular in the U.S. in the last decade and has recently begun to surface in Canada, primarily in the pages of *The Globe and Mail*. In a recent series on the education system, the *Globe* picked up on many of the privatization themes familiar south of the border. In one feature, it trumpeted the story of Laurier Heights, an Edmonton elementary and junior high school which has saved itself from debt and moral decay "by using some of the business and marketing techniques normally associated with the highly competitive private-school system." The article explained that the Edmonton Public School District is one of the few in Canada where parents are free to send their children to any school in the city. Each school's grant from the school board is determined by the number of children who choose to attend, thereby opening up a "free-market approach to education" where schools compete to attract children. (Apparently inspired by the example of the Mulroney government, the parents even set up a "deficit-reduction committee," as well as "focus groups" to examine the school's priorities.)

The *Globe* was clearly excited about the Edmonton experiment and reported in glowing terms on its front page the improved student morale and academic performance at Laurier Heights. But at the end of the article, on the bottom of page 10, reporter Miro Cernetig revealed some of the problems with this new approach. He quoted parents as saying that the free market system leaves schools competing for a limited number of pupils and raiding each other, thereby leaving some schools with reduced funds. And, while Laurier Heights is theoretically open to all pupils, in practice, the majority come from the affluent area where the school is located. As a result, more public money ends up going to a school in a well-to-do suburb, attended primarily by children in the neighbourhood, at the expense of schools elsewhere in the city. Cernetig notes that at Laurier Heights, "Jaguars and BMWs are not uncommon sights," and that many mothers in the area do not have jobs and are willing to give generous amounts of their time to help out in the classroom or with school administration. Cernetig comments that this may not be the case in other city neighbourhoods.

Indeed, this free market approach to education carries the potential for significant inequalities, as we can see south of the border, where much of the public school system has been remodelled along these free market lines. The Bush administration was particularly keen on promoting the concept of "schools of choice," where certain schools become "magnets," attracting the brightest students from throughout the district by offering excellent facilities, teaching staff and high standards. While these "magnet" schools are theoretically open to all students, they are generally located in affluent areas and throw up many subtle and not-so-subtle obstacles to admission, such as entrance tests and application forms. As Jonathan Kozol demonstrates in his study of the U.S. school system, poor parents often lack the education and initiative to prepare their children for the necessary tests and line up the required forms and recommendations needed for admission. In the final analysis, admission is controlled by the number of spaces, and well-to-do, well-connected parents often have the inside track in getting their children into the limited spaces available at the better schools.

In some situations, the discrimination is more blatant. In Chicago, parents in a middle-income condominium development called Dearborn Park wanted to keep children from a local housing project out of a beautiful new elementary school built in the neighbourhood in the late '80s. The Dearborn Park parents arranged with the school board not to admit the housing project children to the school until Grade Three, allowing their children a substantial head start. According to *The New York Times*, the children from the housing project were instead required to spend the first three years of their elementary education attending "a small, prefabricated metal building surrounded on three sides by junkyards."

So, while the free market approach to education may seem to offer quick-fix solutions, it does so at a price. Kozol notes that Bush's "schools of choice" system — a variation of which is being tried in Edmonton — involves a trade-off between the freedom of parents to create enclaves of excellence for their own children and the rights of children who end up in less well funded schools. These unlucky children end up "even more isolated," says the Chicago *Tribune,* because they end up separated from the more successful students, as well as being left out of the better schools.

For Canadians, the U.S. stands as a chilling example of what the future may hold for us. While there are many admirable aspects of American democracy, the growing inequality in American society should act as a warning signal to Canadians who do not want to see such inequality in our own society. Larry Mishel of Washington's Economic Policy Institute says that the U.S. is already on its way to becoming two societies — a prosperous élite and a huge underclass of working and non-working poor.

One theme that clearly emerges when we look at the more advanced social welfare systems of western Europe is the strong, positive role played by government. But here in Canada we have increasingly come to believe that government spending is too high. Indeed, business has spooked many of us into believing that big government is the problem, and that we must strip government of much of its power and resources and hand them to the private marketplace. It is this approach — this emphasis on the private market solution — that is whittling away our social welfare system.

Canada, like the European countries, has traditionally spent generously in the areas of health care and education, but we have been considerably less generous in our spending on job training, on day care and on government payments for pensions, family benefits and housing allowances. As a result, Europeans tend to have a stronger floor of support beneath them that prevents them from falling into poverty in the first place, and entering into that prison of deprivation and despair in which so many American and Canadian families are trapped.

Here are some specific recommendations of how we can realistically apply some of the lessons of Europe to Canada.

## * Our social welfare system should be universal.

The Europeans have made greater gains in social welfare largely because they have involved the whole society: in essence, everyone pays, everyone benefits and everyone feels part of the system. This inclusive approach appears to provide the best hope of providing decent living standards for all, as well as widespread support for the system.

Canadians should therefore resist suggestions by business and government that we target our resources exclusively at the poor. While this approach sounds sensible and fair, it is fraught with problems, as we have seen. Not only does it stigmatize the poor, but it easily leads to resentment on the part of those who pay taxes and receive no benefits. Instead, we should follow the European example and provide strong universal systems, with *additional* benefits available to those with special needs.

Thus, we should re-establish and strengthen our universal family allowance program, which Ottawa killed this year after whittling away at it for years. This program was originally established to provide a floor of support for Canadian families, and to prevent them from becoming dependent on public relief and private charity in tough economic times. But while the Europeans have maintained generous family allowances over the years — and coupled them with housing allowances in many countries — we have allowed ours to diminish and now to disappear, leaving us without family or housing allowances. The spectacle of hundreds of thousands of Canadians lining up at food banks is a commentary on how badly we need a program to help families pay for the most basic necessities.

There is also an urgent need to protect universality in health care and higher education. Massive federal cutbacks have threatened to destroy the egalitarian nature of these two crucial systems, which have traditionally made up the impressive part of our social welfare system. As provincial governments try to make up for lost federal revenues with user fees in health care and higher tuition fees at post-secondary institutions, we risk developing two-tiered systems, with the better facilities and services available to those with greater financial resources.

\* **We should establish a universal day-care program.**
Clearly, one of our most pressing social problems is child poverty. According to the National Council of Welfare, there are 1.1 million Canadian children growing up poor — roughly one in six. The problem exists right across the country and is increasingly being relegated to private solutions like food banks. The long-term implications of this poverty are dramatic, not just for the deprived children but for Canadian society as a whole as these children enter adulthood with a sense of having been left out of the mainstream of Canadian life.

There are clearly many causes of child poverty, from high unemployment to lack of effective family support programs. But the lack of affordable day care is a key part of the problem, particularly for single-mother families, which make up a growing segment of the poor. There are now 440,000 children growing up poor in such families — an increase from 328,000 in 1980. Without access to day care, single mothers are unable to work and are therefore left with no means of support other than meagre welfare benefits.

But there is an acute shortage of licensed day-care spaces — only enough for 13 per cent of the total number of children whose parents work outside the home, according to the National Council of Welfare. While day-care subsidies are theoretically available for poor families, the lack of available spaces creates a Catch-22; if there are no available spaces in the area, parents cannot receive the subsidy, even if they qualify. A study prepared for Ottawa's Special Committee on Child Care found that only 15 per cent of those eligible for a full or partial subsidy actually received assistance in 1987.

Furthermore, in an era of global competition, a national day-care program — along with a well-funded education system — is surely a wise investment in the future. As the child-care experts on the French-American study tour observed in their report, children who receive good early childhood education are more likely to do well in school later. Thus, an investment in child care now is likely to pay off later by producing a better-educated citizenry. If we are serious about making our country globally competitive, we should begin by investing now in our most important resource — our future workforce.

**\* We should make gender equality a top priority.**

A quick look at Canadian poverty statistics reveals the predominance of women — 59 per cent — among Canada's poor. While a national day-care program would help this situation by allowing more women to work, the inequities women face in the job market are another large part of the problem.

Female poverty is heavily concentrated among unattached women — with or without children. Married women have very low poverty rates, because they can count on their husband's income. But for women who must support themselves — whether divorced, widowed or never-married — poverty rates are dramatically above the national average for all Canadians.

All this points to the need for greater equality in the job market. Although two-thirds of Canadian women now work, mostly in full-time jobs, their pay continues to be dramatically less than men's pay. According to the UN, women in Canada earn 63 per cent of what men earn, whereas French women earn 82 per cent, and Swedish women 89 per cent. (U.S. women, by contrast, earn only 59 per cent of their male counterparts.) As a result, Canadian women continue to be overrepresented at the bottom of the income ladder: females represented more than 60 per cent of Canadians earning less than $10,000 a year and less than 20 per cent of those earning more than $100,000 a year, according to Revenue Canada statistics.

The wage gap is a significant contributor to the poverty of both women and children and should be addressed directly through stronger equal pay laws and more affirmative action programs, not vague expressions of concern. As Daniel Drache and John O'Grady observed in *Getting On Track*: "Scandinavian employers do not pay women workers wages that are virtually the same as those of male workers because they share a commitment to gender equality; rather they do so because those are the rules."

* **We should make fighting unemployment a top priority.**

Ottawa has stressed the importance of reducing inflation, but has put little emphasis on reducing unemployment. As a result, inflation has dropped significantly, but unemployment hovers above 11 per cent.

This represents enormous personal suffering for the 1.6 million unemployed Canadians, who must now support themselves and their families on greatly reduced incomes. The unemployed also find the safety net beneath them suddenly weaker: unemployment benefits have been cut back, and federal payments to the provinces to cover welfare costs have been reduced, causing municipal governments to cut welfare spending. A 1991 parliamentary subcommittee on poverty noted that there is "a clear relationship between the rates of unemployment and child poverty."

Furthermore, high unemployment places enormous strain on the country's financial resources and ultimately, therefore, on its ability to pay for its social programs. Not only do we lose potential tax revenue from unemployed Canadians, but our social insurance systems are stretched as we provide additional benefits to more and more desperate families.

Job creation and job training have traditionally been areas where Canada, compared to other advanced nations, has a weak record. And, despite the massive job loss and dislocation caused by its Free Trade Agreement, the Conservative government has done little to retrain the Canadian workforce and rebuild the Canadian economy. At the same time, it has removed the obligation for the federal government to contribute to the unemployment insurance fund, thereby further reducing Ottawa's involvement in the task of lowering unemployment.

Any effort to improve the welfare of Canadians should begin with policies that put the goal of full employment at the top of the political agenda.

**\* We should reform our social programs — not with the goal of cutting their costs — but with the goal of making them more effective and cost-efficient.**

Most of the changes to our social programs have been made in response to business demands for spending cuts. This approach creates serious problems as it moves us towards a U.S.-style welfare system. But opposing this approach does not mean we should uncritically accept our social programs as they are. On the contrary, we must find more effective ways to spend our resources to improve the social welfare of Canadians.

Dr. Michael Rachlis notes that while we spend a great deal on health care, we seem to be losing sight of our goal: to improve the health of Canadians.

Rachlis says that we spend too much on doctors, drugs and high-tech medical equipment providing "bypass surgery for the boys."

If we really want to improve the health of Canadians, says Rachlis, we should cut back spending in these areas and increase spending on basic measures that will ensure children are born healthy in the first place. Thus, the key is to improve the health and economic status of young women, he says, since unhealthy, undernourished women are more likely to give birth to unhealthy babies, with long-term health implications.

* **We should reform our tax system to make it fairer.**

A good social welfare system is costly to maintain, and taxpayers will only be willing to pay for it if they feel that everyone is contributing their fair share. Certainly, any serious attempt to address the problem of government spending and the deficit must include a careful assessment of whether our tax system is allowing some Canadians to avoid making an adequate contribution to the community.

Tax expert Neil Brooks notes that Canada and Australia are the only countries in the advanced capitalist world that have no inheritance tax, thereby allowing fortunes to pass untaxed from one generation to another. As we've seen, Brooks has identified a series of tax breaks that cost the Canadian treasury more than $8 billion a year — and primarily benefit business and the rich. He says that we could scrap them without harming the economy. Brooks argues, for instance, that we could easily abolish the business entertainment deduction which costs us more than $1 billion a year in lost revenues.

Canadians should shun the temptations of a tax revolt. While low taxes are appealing, they inevitably constrain the ability of governments to provide adequate social programs. Right-wing organizations in Canada — like the National Citizens' Coalition and the Fraser Institute — have long tried to encourage a U.S.-style tax revolt in Canada as part of their efforts to dismantle the Canadian social welfare system.

Tax revolts, despite their populist overtones, largely benefit the rich. Reducing the tax base limits the society's ability to provide social welfare for its citizens — something of little importance to the rich, who generally prefer to buy their own high-quality services privately anyway, but of immense importance to the rest of society. Says James Laxer: "If you want to destroy a society, set low tax rates."

Rather than demanding lower taxes, Canadians should be demanding fairer taxes and a better social welfare system.

Any assessment of the future of the welfare state should include an acknowledgement of the major role it has played in improving the quality of life for millions of people throughout the industrialized world. The notion that people are born with inherent social rights as citizens — rights to health care and education and a decent standard of living — is a far cry from the minimal concept of citizenship that existed as recently as the last century, indeed, during the first few decades of this century and still today throughout much of the underdeveloped world. The egalitarian thrust of the welfare state is almost unique in recent human history.

The rise of the welfare state — which really began in earnest in the '40s — has dramatically changed the way we in the industrialized world live and divide up the resources of our societies. Although it has advanced further in some countries than in others, there has been dramatic progress in only a few short decades in most of the West, and in parts of the less-developed world as well. By 1983, 130 countries had some form of old-age and disability benefits, 85 countries offered maternity and sickness benefits, 40 countries offered unemployment insurance and 67 countries offered family allowances. The effect of all these programs on human well-being has been dramatic. Comments OECD analyst Edwin Bell: "If you look at OECD countries at the time of the Second World War, all these [social welfare] systems were underdeveloped. Now in all countries there is a complex of programs, and everyone expects them. That's what we call the welfare state. With any huge system obviously there's always debates and arguments, but the bottom line is a success story. That is where we should start. We've removed poverty, ill-health and insecurity from a lot of people."

As Canadians ponder the future of our social welfare programs, we would be well advised not to get sidelined by the question of whether we can *afford* the welfare state. With the second-highest per capita purchasing power in the world, Canadians can clearly afford a significant welfare state — just as many advanced countries do.

The real question is: Are we willing to pay for one? And that really comes down to this question: How much do we value equality? Do we care if we live in a two-tiered society, with a comfortable élite and a deprived and angry poor?

This is increasingly what we see south of the border. For Canadians, this spectacle has little appeal. Indeed, we seem to have developed a more egalitarian tradition than our southern neighbours — perhaps because we have stronger ties to Europe, or perhaps, as some have suggested, because our colder weather forces us to pool our resources to survive, or, who knows, perhaps just by accident. For whatever reason, a distaste for inequality seems to have become something of a Canadian trait.

Yet with the more advanced welfare states of western Europe an increasingly distant and forgotten model, we are perhaps in greater danger than we realize of replicating the U.S. model here in Canada. Unless we make a clear choice to change our course, we may find ourselves drifting to where we don't really want to go.

# REFERENCES

Aaron, Henry J., *Serious and Unstable Condition.* Washington: Brookings Institution, 1991.

Banting, Keith, "The Welfare State and Inequality in the 1980s," in *The Canadian Review of Sociology and Anthropology.* Vol. 24 (3). 1987.

Bliss, Michael, "Get-Well Canards," in *The Globe and Mail Report on Business Magazine.* Sept. 1991.

Brooks, Neil, *Searching for an Alternative to the GST.* Ottawa: Institute for Research on Public Policy, February 1990.

Brooks, Neil and Doob, Anthony N., "Day care: Helping the rich help themselves," in *The Toronto Star*, March 4, 1992.

Caledon Institute of Social Policy, *Child Benefit Primer.* Ottawa, 1992.

Canada, Department of Finance, *A New Direction for Canada: An Agenda for Economic Renewal.* Ottawa, Nov. 8, 1984.

Canada, Department of Finance, *Economic Review:*

*April, 1980*. Presented by the Hon. Allan J. MacEachen, Minister of Finance.

Canadian Manufacturers' Association, *A Fiscal Strategy for a Balanced Budget in 1994–95: A Pre-Budget Submission to the Hon. Michael H. Wilson*, Feb. 1990.

Center on Budget and Policy Priorities, *The States and the Poor: How Budget Decisions in 1991 Affected Low Income People*. Washington: 1991.

Cernetig, Miro, "Edmonton school overcomes ills of Canadian system," in *The Globe and Mail*, Dec. 28, 1992.

Courchene, Thomas J., *Social Policy in the 1990s: Agenda for Reform*. Toronto: C.D. Howe Institute. Policy Study No. 3, 1987.

————, "Toward the Reintegration of Social and Economic Policy," in G. Bruce Doern and Bryne B. Purchase (eds.), *Canadian Public Policy in the 1990s*. Toronto: C.D. Howe Institute. Policy Study No. 13, 1991.

Cohen, Toby, "Busting the Myths About Canada's Health Care," in *The Wall Street Journal*. Feb. 6, 1992.

Crane, David, "Canadian incomes top U.S. but poverty far from beaten," in *The Toronto Star*. Jan. 30, 1992.

Damus, S., *Canada's Public Sector: A Graphic Overview*. Ottawa: Economic Council of Canada, 1992.

Drache, Daniel (ed.), *Getting on Track: Social Democratic Strategies for Ontario*. Montreal and Kingston: McGill-Queen's University Press, 1992.

Duncan, Greg, et al. *Poverty and Social Assistance Dynamics in the United States, Canada and Europe*. Washington: Joint Center for Political and Economic Studies, 1991.

Enchin, Harvey, "Canada downgraded in competitiveness report," in *The Globe and Mail*. June 22, 1992.

Enthoven, Alain C., "What can Europeans learn from Americans?" in *Health Care Systems in Transition*. Paris: OECD Social Policy Studies, No. 7, 1990.

Evans, Robert G. and Barer, Morris L., "The American predicament," in *Health Care Systems in Transition*. Paris: OECD Social Policy Studies, No. 7, 1990.

Esping-Andersen, Gosta, *The Three Worlds of Welfare Capitalism*. Princeton: Princeton University Press, 1990.

Gairdner, William D., *The War Against the Family*. Toronto: Stoddart, 1992.

Germany, Ministry of Labour and Social Affairs, *Social Security*. Bonn, February 1992.

Gray, Grattan, "Social Policy by Stealth," in *Policy Options*. March, 1990.

Heller, P.S., Hemming, R. and Kohnert, P.W., *Aging and Social Expenditures in the Major Industrial Countries 1980–2025.* Occasional Paper No. 47, International Monetary Fund, Washington, D.C., September 1986.

International Labour Office, *The Cost of Social Security. 13th International Inquiry, 1984–86.* Geneva.

Kamerman, Sheila B., "Child Care Policies and Programs: An International Overview," in *Journal of Social Issues*, Vol. 47, No. 2, 1991.
————, "Toward a Child Policy Decade," in *Child Welfare*, Vol. LXVIII, No. 4, July–Aug. 1989.
————, "Starting Right: What We Owe to Children Under Three," in *The American Prospect*, Winter 1991.
————, "Doing Better by Children: Focus on Families," in *The Journal of Law and Politics*, Vol. VIII, No. 1, Fall 1991.
———— and Kahn, Alfred J., "The Possibilities for Child and Family Policy: A Cross-National Perspective," in Frank J. Macchiarola and Alan Gartner (eds.) *Caring for America's Children.* New York: The Academy of Political Science, 1989.
———— and Kahn, Alfred J., "Family Income Maintenance in Industrialized Societies," in *Public Policy Across Nations: Social Welfare in Industrialized Settings.* JAI Press Inc., 1985.

————— and Kahn, Alfred J., "Single-parent, female-headed families in Western Europe: Social change and response," in *International Social Security Review*. 1/89. Year XLII.

————— and Kahn, Alfred J., "Enhancing the Welfare State" in *The Journal of the Institute for Socioeconomic Studies*, Vol. X, No. 4, Winter 1986.

Korpi, Walter, *The Development of the Swedish Welfare State in Comparative Perspective*. Stockholm: The Swedish Institute, 1990.

—————, "Economic Growth and the Welfare System: Leaky Bucket or Irrigation System?" in *European Sociological Review*, Vol. 1, No. 2, September 1985.

Kozol, Jonathan, *Savage Inequalities: Children in America's Schools*. New York: HarperPerennial, 1992.

Laxer, James, *Inventing Europe*. Toronto: Lester Publishing, 1991.

Marsh, L., Report on Social Security for Canada. (Re-edited version of 1943 original.) Toronto: University of Toronto Press, 1975.

McCord, Colin and Freeman, Harold, "Excess Mortality in Harlem," in *The New England Journal of Medicine*, Vol. 322, No. 3, Jan. 18, 1990.

Monsour, Theresa, "Child-Care Troubles." A special

reprint section in the *Saint Paul Pioneer Press*. Nov. 1991.

Moss, Peter, *Childcare in the European Communities, 1985–1990*. European Commission Childcare Network, August 1990.

Murphy, B.B. and Wolfson, M.C., "When the baby boom grows old: Impacts on Canada's public sector," in *Statistical Journal of the United Nations Economic Commission for Europe*, Vol. 8 (1991).

Muszynski, Leon, *Universality and Selectivity: The Social and Political Ideas and the Policy Issues*. Paper for the Ontario Premier's Council on Health, Well-being and Social Justice. May 1992.

Myles, John and Quadagno, Jill, *Explaining the Difference: The Politics of Old Age Security in Canada and the United States*. Paper for conference, A North American Look at Economic Security for the Elderly. Yale University, May 1991.

Nasar, Sylvia, "Where Did All That 1980s' Wealth Go? Mainly to the Richest 1% of Americans," from the New York Times Service, reprinted in *The International Herald Tribune*, March 6, 1992.

National Council of Welfare, *The 1989 budget and social policy*. Ottawa: Government of Canada, Sept. 1989.

————, *Funding health and higher education: danger looming*. Ottawa: Government of Canada, Spring 1991.

————, *Women and poverty revisited*. Ottawa: Government of Canada, Summer 1990.

————, *Poverty Profile, 1980–1990*. Ottawa: Government of Canada, Autumn 1992.

————, *Child Care: A Better Alternative*. Ottawa: Government of Canada, December 1988.

Navarro, Vicente, "Class and Race: Life and Death Situations," in *Monthly Review*. Sept. 1991.

————, "Why Some Countries Have National Health Insurance, Others Have National Health Services, and the United States has Neither," in *International Journal of Health Services*, Vol. 19, No. 3, 1989.

O'Connor, Julia S. "Welfare expenditure and policy orientation in Canada in comparative perspective," in *Canadian Review of Sociology and Anthropology*, 26(1), 1989.

Organisation for Economic Co-operation and Development, *OECD Economic Outlook, Historical Statistics, 1960–1989*. Paris: OECD, 1991.

Osberg, Lars (ed.), *Economic Inequality and Poverty: International Perspectives*. London: M.E. Sharpe, Inc., 1991.

Pauly, Mark V., "Why is American Health Care So Hard to Reform?" in *The American Enterprise*, Vol. 3, No. 1, Jan-Feb. 1992. Published by the American Enterprise Institute.

Rachlis, Michael, and Kushner, Carol, *Second Opinion*. Toronto: Harper Collins, 1989.

Rachlis, Michael, *The Impact of the 1991 Federal Budget on Health Care, Public Health Programs and the Health Status of Ontario Citizens*. Submission to the Board of Health, City of Toronto. May 1991.

*Report of the Royal Commission on the Economic Union and Development Prospects for Canada*, Vols. 1, 2. Ottawa, 1985.

Richardson, Gail and Marx, Elisabeth, *A Welcome for Every Child: The Report of the Child Care Study Panel of the French-American Foundation*. New York: The French-American Foundation, 1989.

Rothstein, Bo, "The Crisis of the Swedish Social Democrats and the Future of the Universal Welfare State." Paper presented at the Center for European Studies, Harvard University, April 16, 1992.

Schieber, George J. and Poullier, Jean-Pierre, "International Health Spending: Issues and Trends," in *Health Affairs*, Spring 1991.

Schultz, Ellen E., "Working Your Way Through Benefits Puzzle," in *The Wall Street Journal*, Nov. 20, 1992.

Sen, Amartya, "What Did You Learn in the World Today?" in *American Behavioral Scientist*, Vol. 34, No. 5, May/June 1991.

Smeeding, Timothy M. and Rainwater, Lee, *Cross-

*national Trends in Income Poverty and Dependency: The Evidence for Young Adults in the Eighties*. Washington: Joint Center for Political and Economic Studies, 1991.

Spillane, Margaret and Shapiro, Bruce, "The Battle for Public Schools," in *The Nation*. New York, Sept. 21, 1992.

Standing, Guy, *Labor Insecurity Through Market Regulation: Legacy of the 1980s, Challenge for the 1990s*. Washington: Joint Center for Political and Economic Studies, 1991.

Statistics Canada, *Income Distributions by Size in Canada 1991*. Ottawa, 1992.

Swift, Jamie, "Bush Whacked," in *This Magazine*, Oct.-Nov. 1992.

Thorsell, William, "The cult of righteousness flourishes in Canada's rich soil of guilt," in *The Globe and Mail*, Dec. 19, 1992.

Social Planning Council of Metropolitan Toronto and Child Poverty Action Group, *Unequal Futures. The Legacies of Child Poverty in Canada*. Toronto: Social Planning Council of Metropolitan Toronto, 1991.

United Nations, *Human Development Report 1992*. Oxford University Press, 1992. Published for the UN Development Programme.

United States General Accounting Office, *Canadian*

*Health Insurance: Lessons for the United States.*
Washington, June 1991.

Walkom, Thomas, "PM's chart on debt fudged the truth," in *The Toronto Star*, Feb. 12, 1992.

Webber, Marlene, *Food for Thought*. Toronto: Coach House Press, 1992.

Whyte, James L., "Free-market mandarins in the making," in *The Globe and Mail*, Jan. 6, 1993.

Woolhandler, Steffie and Himmelstein, David, "The Deteriorating Administrative Efficiency of the U.S. Health Care System," in *The New England Journal of Medicine*, Vol. 324, No. 18, May 2, 1991.

World Bank, *World Development Report 1991*. Oxford University Press, 1991. Published for the World Bank.

Yalnizyan, Armine, Ritchie, Laurell and McBane, Michael, "Rewriting UI rules doesn't make sense," in *The Globe and Mail*, Feb. 1, 1990.